ROUGH ROADS

Dyke Welkinson

1912

ROUGH ROADS

REMINISCENCES OF A WASTED LIFE

BY

DYKE WILKINSON

LONDON

SAMPSON LOW, MARSTON & CO., LTD.

PREFACE

" A WASTED LIFE," which I published ten years ago, was received equally well by the public and the press. Many private letters, received at the time, show that my readers were found in paths widely apart. Well-known leaders in the religious world assured me the book was good and tended to do good; some belonging to the highest places in the world of sport, and others at the bottom of it, told me they had got no end of amusement out of it. The same may be said of the press. In religious journals there were columns of favourable notices, and prominent preachers made me and my " Wasted Life " the subject of sermons, whilst in all the principal sporting papers there were leading articles and many columns of nothing but praise for it. Here my " Life " was amusing—a comedy. There, the saddest of human documents—a tragedy. So I found myself in the unique position of pleasing people who, in opinion and practice, were poles asunder. As far as I know only one very mild complaint appeared, which was that I said too little about myself in pages teeming with human character of the strangest sort. In " Rough Roads," while I have utilised a good deal of the material of " A

Wasted Life," I have tried to make amends for this mistake, and have said more of myself and much less of others. " A Wasted Life " was often called " A Human Document " ; this book, whatever may be its faults, shall certainly deserve that title. In the preface to " A Wasted Life " I said I had arrived at an age when praise or blame mattered little ; that was written more than ten years ago. How much less, then, shall it matter to-day ? Few writers have dealt so faithfully with themselves as I have done with myself in these pages, and I cannot but wonder what some of my genteel friends and acquaintances will say when they read them.

HIGHGATE, N.,
    September, 1912.

CONTENTS

CHAPTER I

ROUGH ROADS

CHAPTER I

My childhood—In "the Hungry Forties"—Learning to ride—
My first visit to a racecourse, and how I got there—My first
and almost only day school—A rich relation dies—My
father buys a pub.—My education progresses there

Born in the good old town of Birmingham, it is nearly
seventy-five years ago since I gathered my first buttercups
and daisies and chased butterflies in Hickenbotham's
Fields, off New Town Road. Where those fields were
a church was built (has since decayed and been rebuilt),
and to-day the whole locality is a wilderness of dingy
houses and huge manufactories, begrimed, as of age,
and unwholesome ugliness of all sorts, and the nearest
buttercups and daisies are miles and miles away.

I believe my very earliest recollection is of sitting on
my father's shoulder when I was taken to see the first
train arrive in Birmingham in 1838; this will be, I
fear, giving myself away in the matter of age; which,
however, is a slight thing in view of the certainty that,
to make this a human document, I shall have to do it
many times during these truthful chronicles of a wasted
life. I do not remember much of the train, but I quite

B

distinctly remember my father holding me tightly by the legs as he struggled with the surging mass of people around us. My next recollection, I think, would be when most of the poor little children of our neighbourhood were gathered together in a large room, and regaled with currant buns and mugs of milk, or tea, in honour of the marriage of Queen Victoria.

Few of these very early memories are as vividly retained as those that gather about my mother's baking day. Looking back more than two-thirds of a century I see her, a strong rosy-faced woman, scarcely yet middle-aged, her arms bared to the elbows, a huge earthenware vessel, called in those times, a jowl, on a bench in front of her ; and she busy kneading the " batch," which was to make a week's bread for her large family. Then I remember how I trotted behind her and one of my elder brothers, as they bore it in spotless white bags, to the public bakehouse. There I was immensely interested watching her cut it up into great lumps, thumping and banging, and, ultimately, moulding it into the shape of a loaf, such as one never sees in these days, and after marking each one with her own mark she hands them over to the baker, and later in the evening a small procession of us would be seen bearing them in triumph back home, brown and sweet and hot, and when they were placed on the red-tiled floor of our living-room, they reached from one end of it to the other, and how sweet it was to pinch a " puff crumb " off the corner of one of them, and eat it while it was smoking hot. One of these loaves would be worth two, or, perhaps, three shillings, and they were sweet and wholesome to the last bit of them. While the mill-bread, less than half the size, then selling at about a shilling a loaf, stunk when two days old.

This would be in the very early days of " the Hungry Forties."

In those days the butcher's boy, tearing along on his swift steed, was my hero, and so early was I fired with an ambition to learn to ride. No horse was available or donkey even ; so one day, after my father had gone to work, I invaded the large " sty " in our little garden, where he kept the pig, and mounting its back, careered several times around the outer part of the sty. Now whether the pig failed to appreciate the sport, or wanted to lie down, I don't know, anyway, he made a sudden bolt through the narrow passage to his bed, and I was left outside, unconscious, and on my forehead a memento of my first efforts in the art of riding which remains there to this day. This untoward beginning did not cure me of my determination to learn to ride ; so I frequently found my way to Brick-kiln Fields in Summer Lane, near my home, and then quite in the country. On the west side of the lane there were, I should say, hundreds of acres of unenclosed land, where people were allowed to " turn out " any kind of animal for grazing, the only building there being a small saw mill, with great stacks of felled trees and baulks of timber, waiting their turn for the mill. Hard by were two large pools of water, one stocked with bulrushes, and the other with fish, mostly

" Jack Bannels " or minnow.   These lands stretched away over the " Sandy Hill " nearly to the Lozel's, and was the playground of all the youngsters at my end of the town.

Some delighted in hunting the butterfly and beautiful moths, which were plentiful here ; some played " tick " among the timbers ; some, with their hands, scooped minnow from the pool and took them home in bottles ; while others gathered the pretty bulrushes. None of these simple sports, however, charmed me. The grazing animals claimed most of my attention. I annexed a slice of my mother's clothes-line, and made a halter, then hieing to the Brick-kiln Fields, would capture first a donkey, and, later on, horses, and ride till I tumbled off, or until (as more than once happened) I was myself captured and well thrashed. But this looking like the only possible way of realising my ambition to learn to ride, the thrashings didn't stop me. Thus, early in my life, I developed a passion for horses, which, like other human passions have

" Oft-times led me wrong."

Horses have afforded me a great deal of pleasure, and occasionally some profit ; but what with broken ribs, legs, arms, and pocket, I have not found my love for them " a joy for ever," or my dealings with them an unmixed pleasure. One of my earliest experiences of the noble animal was in the year—well, never mind the year, it is farther behind me than I care to realise. I had come across a horse straying about the streets without bridle, saddle, or halter, so I drove him into the yard in the rear of my father's house, and improvising a halter out of the old clothes-line, was on the way with him to the nearest "pound"; where they took charge of him, handing a ticket to me which was my warrant for a shilling, to be received when the horse was claimed. However, instead of receiving a shilling, I got one of the soundest of all my thrashings. The horse was the property of a small tradesman, an intimate friend of my father, and it appeared some mischievous boys had driven him out of a badly-fenced field, where he was grazing. The owner explained to my father the circumstances, and assured him I was one of the culprits—this time, however, he was mistaken—so I not only lost my shilling, but I got a thrashing which caused me to vow that none of my good actions in the future should consist of taking care of other people's stray horses.

It was also in these very tender years that I got my first experience of a race meeting, which came about in this way.

John Dyke, in those days, was a notable betting man, made a book, owned racers of his own, and was as George Payne and other ancient turfites have related to me, a man of some account on the turf, in the thirties and forties of the last century. It happened that this same John Dyke, my mother's brother, was, while a young man, troubled with ambitions to be something other than a journeyman button maker, so had taken to the making of books, which resulted in his leaving Birmingham and living at London in some style.

Once a year this great man of our family came down to Wolverhampton races. And I know that the less fortunate members of the family whom he had left behind him in Birmingham, looked forward to these annual visits of " Uncle John " with a great deal of pleasure ; and I am sure they had substantial reasons for looking back to them with gratitude, for he was a true racing man, and whatever his faults, had a big heart and an open hand.

In those days the facilities for travelling between Birmingham and Wolverhampton were very different to what they are now. Many did the thirteen miles on " Shanks' pony," while for others every conceivable sort of vehicle was pressed into service. My father used to hire our vegetable merchant's " spring " cart, and in this stowed away my mother and eight or ten members of the family or friends.

I suppose I should be seven years old when I took it into my head that it was time I was included in the party ; and I remember how I howled when told that my time, for that sort of thing, was not yet. They started gaily on their journey ; I raced after them, and but for an untoward circumstance, should, I believe, have overtaken the lumbering old horse which carried them in the " spring " cart to the races.

A sister, fleet of foot and thrice my age, who had been left in charge, pursued me, seized me by the " scruff of the neck," and dragging me back home, shut me up in the bedroom ; and to make quite sure I shouldn't make a second attempt, despoiled me of my cap and jacket.

This, however, did not stop me ; and half an hour after—bare-headed and jacketless—I was trudging along the Wolverhampton Road, which was lively all the way with motley crowds bound for the races. My goal was " Uncle John." By dint of hard walking, stealing an occasional ride hanging on to passing traps, I managed to get to Wolverhampton ; got down to the crowded race grounds, but, of course, got no glimpse of this miraculous uncle, or of my father and mother.

When the races were over, tired and very hungry—and helped by bigger boys—I found my way back to the highway, intending to trudge back to Birmingham. I had not travelled very far before I got a glimpse of something a hundred yards or so in front of me, which gave me more delight than anything I had seen that day. It was a peculiar cashmere shawl, which my mother was wearing. I knew she was wrapped in that shawl, but I was far too done up to run after her.

" That's my father and mother," I cried to the biggest of my companions, pointing them out to him. " You go and stop them, and you'll get a lift."

He rushed after them, overtook them, and they halted till I arrived on the scene, then I was dragged into the cart, my friend attempting to follow me, but the " lift " he got was from the instrument with which my father was endeavouring to urge on the jaded horse with already a too heavy load. There was no space for me to sit, but I was very glad to lie among their feet at the bottom of the trap, where I soon fell asleep.

I remember that, when a child, I had frequently to walk all the way from the bottom of Brearley Street, carrying a large bottle, to the spring at the corner of Steward Street in Spring Hill, hundreds of people, from all parts of Birmingham, making pilgrimage there for the same purpose, to get the water, which was said to be a cure for bad eyes. I suppose the distance would be four miles ; and it was no light task for a little chap of seven to trudge that distance loaded with a heavy bottle. Some portion of my way was through green fields and pleasant lanes. These, with the magic spring, disappeared long years ago, and what that densely populated district is now, Birmingham people know. Another long journey in an opposite direction was necessary whenever any shoemending was needed, which was all too often in a large family of lads. Our shoemaker lived in Watery Lane, which was then a real country lane with cornfields near at hand ; and in the autumn I have many a time done some "leasing" in these fields. One incident connected with these visits to the old snobbery is still clear in my memory, although it is about seventy years ago. I was sent about mid-day on one occasion, to fetch some boots back from the snobbery, and, instead of going direct to the shoemaker's when I arrived in Watery Lane, I could not resist the temptation to pay a visit to the nearest cornfield, which was in Kingston Lane, lying between what should have been the end of my journey and the highway to London. There I found congenial company. The reapers had just finished their task.

and what with romping with my companions, and gathering a goodly sheaf of corn, I found myself making my way homewards, very tired, burdened with a load of boots, and my sheaf of corn at what time I ought to have been to bed. I was so tired I was obliged to take a rest on the wooden shutter covering the entrance to a cellar of one of the houses I was to pass ; and there, with my head pillowed on the corn, and the boots locked in my arms, I dropped into a sound sleep, dreaming probably of what would happen when I arrived home. Here my father found me, toward midnight, after a long and anxious search. What did happen when I got home, I do not recollect. I have no doubt, however, my reward was similar to those I received for the many escapades of my childhood of a like character, or worse.

Following this came a rather severe illness, which my mother assured me was the result of this very escapade. I have no recollection of what was the nature of the illness, I only remember that an old woman came, and put some leeches on me, which bit me horribly and sucked the blood out of me ; this being, I believe, the principal method of doctoring poor people in those days, for all over the neighbourhood you would see in every street, in the dirty little window of a dirty little house, a glass bottle full of these fearsome wretches, and an execrably scribbled notice that " *Leeches are kept here.*"

I had a good father, perhaps a little too careless and easy for the head of an unusually large family of unruly boys.

That he was a fairly educated man, for one born in the eighteenth century, his handwriting, still in existence, goes to prove ; and the fact that all his brothers, whom I knew, were educated men, in business on their own account ; and his sisters, women of some culture and refinement, tends to confirm the stories he was wont to tell us of his spendthrift father, who was the son of a fine old English yeoman who farmed his own extensive lands in the neighbourhood of Birmingham.

Of my mother it will be enough to say every one of us loved her tenderly during her life, and the few of us who are left revere her memory ; and although since she died, half a century of strenuous life has seared and hardened me in many things, her dear face, and my last glimpse of it, is vivid in my memory as were it a thing of yesterday.

We being a very large family, education, for any of us, was out of the question. I remember I went to a dame's school, in the tiny living room of a small house, somewhere up a dark court in Lower Brearlet Street, and, for a little time, at Bishop Ryder's School. At no time, however, did the outlay on my education exceed twopence a week ; and whatever of useful knowledge I managed to get I began to get for myself when I became a button-cobber at Hammond Turner's in Snow Hill ; my first wage being eighteenpence a week, and this was when I was well under eight years old. I believe I learnt to read by diligent study of the tradesmen's signboards in the streets, to and from my work. When I left Hammond Turner's I went to work at Pemberton's famous brass foundry at an advance of sixpence a week ; the head of that firm was, I should say, grandfather or great-grandfather of a celebrated literary man of the present day owning that ancient and honoured Birmingham name. During my brief school days the sound of the Punch and Judy man's pipes and the sight of his show would lure me to play truant at that time, and it was even so when the more serious matter of work engaged me ; I could not resist the temptation to follow them, and this, occasionally, got me into trouble. Very early in life I had learnt to read, and was greedily absorbing anything and everything that came in my way. The death of a relative brought my father capital to the extent of two or three hundred pounds ; with this he bought a small public-house ; and here I found my education grow apace, while my opportunities for reading were largely increased, my literature being, I fancy, very much mixed.

I was enchanted with a torn and dirty old Bunyan's *Pilgrim's Progress*, and a *Robinson Crusoe*, which I found among the rubbish my father had taken over when he bought the " Dog and Pheasant." With these I found *Jack Sheppard*, *Three-Fingered Jack*, and sundry other tales of a like elevating character.

Nothing, however, in the shape of reading came amiss to me, and all were assimilated with equal zest and impartiality. I am, however, quite sure *Bell's Life in London* was my chief delight.

There was no Birmingham daily paper in those days, and none elsewhere which found its way to the " Dog and

Pheasant." The famous old *Sporting Weekly*, with Aris's *Birmingham Gazette*, and the *Dispatch*, were the first newspapers I became acquainted with. These were " Taken in Here," as a printed card, displayed in the big " bow windows " in front of our house, intimated to all concerned. After these papers had been well read by the " indoors" for a day or two after publication, they travelled all over the neighbourhood from one to another of the " outdoors," and toward the end of the week, much the worse for wear and tear, they found their way back home, and were at my service, and then how eagerly I took in their contents. *Bell* was my prime favourite, especially that part of it which told of the mighty deeds of the gentlemen who were immortalising themselves within the magic circle of the P.R. of those times. Birmingham being the birthplace and school of these heroes, I not only saw their names in real print, but I saw them in real flesh ; actually saw the great men walking about our pavements of petrified kidneys like ordinary mortals. I have even known some of the lesser among those demi-gods—such as Teddy Mush and Jotter Palmer—visit my father's humble hostelry, and seen them take a turn at " Madam Clark " and " Ring the Bull " for quarts of " fourpenny " in our sawdusted taproom.

The great city of Birmingham was, by comparison, a mere village when I was born ; it had, however, begun its marvellous growth, and a few years after it received its charter of incorporation as a borough. Its sickly schoolmaster, Rowland Hill, was pondering over the possibility of delivering letters at the uniform charge of a penny to any part of the country in place of the high rate regulated by the distance they had to travel. I remember that when a child and the rare occasion for my father to write a letter arose I had to trudge all the way from our northern extremity of the town to the shabby little general post-office in New Street.

Mention of Rowland Hill brings to my memory an occasion—I think it must have been in the late forties—when I saw his celebrated brother, Mathew Davenport Hill, who, then Recorder of Birmingham, was trying prisoners at the Sessions held at the old police-court in Moor Street. But it was not to see him I had squeezed myself into the dingy little court. Some one had told me that Lord Byron's widow—Hill's friend, and like him interested in what was then a novel question, the reformation of youthful criminals—was sitting by his side on the Bench, and it was to get a glimpse of her who had been the wife of one of my earliest demi-gods that I was there.

In the hungry forties Birmingham was agitated a good deal with the bread question. The mill-made loaf, which I remember so well, as I have said, not over sweet at its best, awfully sour and almost uneatable when two days old, cost poor people about a shilling. To increase the discontent a rumour got about that the millers were grinding all sorts of horrible bones to mix with the flour; and I remember being present at one of the riots at Snow Hill flour mill when the mob wrecked the place. A respected

family named Rayner owned the mill, and I call to mind
how, many years afterwards, a member of that family, who
sat by my side as a colleague on the King's Norton Board
of Guardians, solemnly assured me there was not a particle
of reason for the rumour as far as their mill was concerned.

Not only in France were the closing years of the forties
notable for huge upheavals of society and political unrest ;
Birmingham was in the throes of the Chartist Movement,
and I remember some of her best men being sent to prison
for using language which, in these days, would be considered quite tame, and for advocating changes nearly all
of which have long since become laws of the land.   More
than once I heard George Edmonds and Arthur O'Niel
speak with enthusiasm of their crime—glorying in their
imprisonment for it.

I have just one other reminiscence of Birmingham in
the Forties which may interest the children of the
present generation.   For years after the good old town
became incorporated it was the custom for the Mayor
and Corporation to open its fair with a public procession
and considerable pomp ; and how present to my mind,
even now, is the figure of the little old town-crier, Jacob
Wilson, in all the glory of cocked hat and ancient uniform,
with the great bell under his arm, marching proudly
in front of the Mayor and other great men, and at stated
intervals stopping to ring it ; then declaring—with the
time-honoured " Oyez ! Oyez! Oyez ! "—that the fair is
now opened.   Then the fair itself, what a wonderful
event it was.   In Dale End stood Wombwell's Wild Beast

Show and sundry smaller shows. All along High Street, the Bull Ring, and right away to Bromsgrove Street, on either side, as closely as they could be packed, were the stalls for the sale of gingerbread and other good things. Where the great vegetable market now stands, and facing Bromsgrove Street, was Patch and Bennett's famous wood and canvas theatre. It had a stage outside where the band played, and where clown, pantaloon, and the gentleman with a million shining spangles on his dress went through a gratuitous performance which was to whet our appetite and wheedle from us the pennies for the show inside.

Then there were the numerous smaller shows where the bearded lady, the fat lady, the two-headed animals, and other monstrosities were on view, all at the same low price.

A notable feature of the fair was the halfpenny rides on wooden horses, and as it was long before the application of steam for the purpose, the boys who lacked the halfpennies pushed them round, taking, for doing this, an occasional ride gratis.

Then there were any quantity of whirligigs and swing-boats, and as the result of venturing on these I have frequently seem something quite as bad as sea-sickness. I suppose the exigencies of the growing traffic and other considerations made it necessary to discontinue these ancient fairs, but I dare say there still remain a few old fogies, like myself, who regret it, and look back to them as days of unalloyed happiness.

CHAPTER II

I am apprenticed—A hard master—How we repaid him—A peep-hole in the wall, and what came of it—Served with a summons—A budding ꞏpoet—I ran away—Adventures as a tramp

A GOOD deal may be said in favour of the system of apprenticing boys at the age of fourteen for seven years, which was the common practice among all trades in Birmingham in my early days. Given conditions which should safeguard the interests of the apprentice as well as the master, I see no reason to object to it. If the number was limited, say one apprentice to each journeyman, the lad would have a fair chance of learning his trade, and, under the daily governance and restraint this condition should impose, he would learn the meaning of the word discipline, learn his trade ; and most likely become a useful member of society. I am quite certain if something of this sort had been done in my case I should have been saved years of misery, and many of my fellow-apprentices an even worse fate, and such disgraceful things as I am about to describe, and other things indescribable, would have been simply impossible.

When twelve and a half years old, I was apprenticed to a rule maker in St. Paul's Square for eight years and a half. Oh! the horrible cruelty of that act. An old, hardened man of the world, I shiver, even now, when I recall all that I saw, and suffered, and did—I was but a child—during the earlier years of that damnable apprenticeship, and my blood boils up, hot and fierce.

There were, as far as my memory serves me, about twenty apprentices, and very few men. No one to control us, teach us our craft, or show us a way to good of any sort. Knowledge of our trade was, for the most part, acquired of our elder fellow-apprentices, or got as best we might. Knowledge of other sort was abundant, and the teachers plentiful. But the sort was bad, and wrought much mischief in the lives of many of these apprentices. Indeed, in my after life, I have wondered how any one of us came through the ordeal of that fatal bondage without being horribly scathed.

When I was bound I was too young to see what I was doing, or to understand the enormity of the sin of which I was the victim, but my eyes were soon open. I saw I was apprenticed to a trade and to surroundings I detested. The irksomeness of it became unbearable, and every fibre of my being revolted. This resulted in a very general revolt among the lads, which, I fear, I was answerable for ; and our employers—there were three of them—an old man and two sons—were not long in discovering they had made a bad bargain when they took me on. The old man and his family lived in a large house in St. Paul's Square ; the factory, with an entrance from Ludgate Hill, being in the rear of it.

c

The particular shop where I worked, with five or six other boys, had once been an attic belonging to the house, and was approached by two flights of steps running up the outside of the house. Connected with our workshop there was a little narrow room where other apprentices were engaged; in this room there was a most convenient window, looking down on the aforesaid steps, so that should we of the larger room be improperly occupied when the governor came bounding up the steps, the others generally heard him, and passed on the arranged signal which enabled us to be busy when he arrived on the scene. This, however, did not always work satisfactorily, for he frequently came up stealthily in his slippers. This so exasperated the lads they took to shying at him rotten potatoes, lumps of stale bread, and, I am ashamed to say, on occasions, things of a worse description. He would threaten, and fume, and cross-question for an hour, but never succeeded in making any one confess which was the culprit.

The elder of the sons, who was the best hated member of the family, would frequently, for some trivial offence, give a boy what we called drill-bow beating; that was, thrashing him with one of his own tools. On one occasion he picked up my drill-bow with an evident intention of putting it about my back. I happened to have in my hand, at the time, a long steel chisel, very sharp, and a long wooden handle attached to it. I fancy he saw something in my eyes he didn't like; anyway, he changed his intention, and, laying the drill-bow on the bench instead of across my back, began to lecture me on my duty to *my masters*. Now, nothing raised my rebellious spirit like this, so I treated him to a little lecture when my turn came ; and, to this day, I have a distinct recollection of the very words I used, " You are no *master* of mine," I said, " but only a man who buys my labour for a good deal less than it's worth." I have often thought what an impudent young rascal I must have been. There came a day, however, when I had to submit to the drill-bow ; and it came about in this way. " Mr. John," as he was called, finding himself thwarted in the matter of spying on us with the aid of his slippers, hit upon an ingenious device for the purpose ; he scooped out the mortar between two of the bricks in the wall which divided our shop from his bedroom ; so providing himself with a neat little peephole, of course immediately behind *me*, and within a few feet of the vice where I worked. This clever device, however, came perilously near being tragical for the author of it. On the bedroom side of it the peephole had a covering of some sort, which gave Mr. John an unfair advantage, because, while he was able to spy on us, we had no chance of seeing what took place on his side of the wall. I stood this peephole business for some time, and then my spirit rebelled against it. I fancied I heard the covering gently removed ; I had a stout piece of iron wire in my hand, about a foot long ; quick as thought I sent the wire through the peephole ; I heard a voice cry " Oh ! " In two minutes Mr. John was flying up the flight of steps outside our shop ; he burst in, beside

himself with rage, and seizing my drill-bow set about
me in real earnest. This lasted only about one minute,
during which I managed to possess myself of what is
known in the trade as " a steady," a heavy article of steel
about three inches square and sharp at all its eight
points. He saw this, and bolted for the door of the narrow
shop adjoining, and, as he reached it, I threw the steady
with all the force I could muster, straight at his head, and
I rejoice that I missed it by about the length of a tooth-
pick, for had my aim, by so little, been truer I should
surely now be burdened with horror that, in my passion,
I had killed a fellow-creature. As long as I knew that
door it bore the certain evidence of that. As the one
pleasant result of this almost tragic incident there was
never more any attempt at thrashing me. Another
result was less pleasant ; I was summoned to answer for
my conduct before the magistrates. The summons was
served on me, while I was at work, by a policeman ;
" Mr. John," with an evil grin on his face, introducing
him. I knew what the paper meant, for I had seen
them served on others of the lads, so I coolly placed it
underneath my feet and went on with my work, only
answering " Mr. John's " ugly grin with the saucy remark
that the summons was where " I would like to have
the man that had sent it." The outcome of all this
was an adventure which I must briefly relate, not only
because it will show the kind of lad I was, but it will
serve to illustrate the pernicious effect of the only literature I was able to come by. But before I relate the sequel

to this summons I shall state a few facts which prove that, amid all the folly and wickedness of this little hell of a workshop, I was trying to be something better than my surroundings.

Even before my apprenticeship, although my educational opportunities were so few, I suppose I must have equipped myself after a fashion, for I remember that I was soon adding something to my scanty earnings by writing love-letters and epistles of all sorts for fellow-workmen much older than myself, and by telling stories to my fellow-apprentices, all of which were manufactured out of my own head as I told them. Five or six of these lads, foregoing the pleasure of dining at home, would bring their allowance for that meal wrapped in dirty bits of newspapers, or dirtier little cotton handkerchiefs, and sit around me, during the dinner hour, while I regaled them with tales of horror and adventure, which, I have no doubt, were the outcome of my study of the dreadful trash which was almost the only literary food for poor lads of that time. For this service each of my listeners subscribed a halfpenny a week.

I was as early as this beginning to fancy myself a poet. In an attic where I and one or two of my brothers slept I nearly covered the whitewashed walls with my effusions in this line, and I remember that one of my brothers, older than myself, and lacking my devotion to the Muses, frequently resented my disturbing him in the very early morning by this scribbling in a manner a deal more forcible than pleasant. In the winter months, instead of disturbing them in the morning, I got into trouble by disturbing them very late at night, while occupied in the same pursuit ; and many a time would my dear old mother leave her bed, steal quietly up to the attic and surprise me ; and I fancy I can hear her voice now, as, despoiling me of my candle, she says, " Get into bed, you foolish boy, wasting your paper and my candles."

And now I must tell how, instead of answering the summons, I determined to run away, go to sea, and be a hero of some sort ; and so had I infused my romantic spirit into a couple of my companions they decided to go with me. The important matter was to get to London, where the streets were paved with gold. Possessing not even the proverbial half-crown with which some great men accomplished wonders ; in fact, without anything in the shape of money, but with high hopes, and any amount of confidence, we started on the quest of fame. I had very bad boots for a trudge of a hundred and twenty odd miles. We might have made the distance less by going *via* Coventry, but I determined to go *via* Stratford-on-Avon because I wanted to see the place where Shakespeare was born ; and Stratford was our haven of rest for the first night, and what sleep we got was on boards in the casual ward of the workhouse there. One of my companions was bigger and older than myself, the other was a rather delicate lad, smaller and younger ; and I remember he cried a good deal in the night and was frightened by the dreadful men, our fellow tramps.

After being served with a basin of skilly and a lump of dry bread for breakfast we got on the road again, and made for Oxford—the small boy crying and the big one grumbling a good deal on the way. We had little to eat this day except some raw turnips we got from a field, but when we reached Oxford we got some sort of a feed, with the casual ward for a lodging. The next day we passed through Henley-on-Thames, and toward night were very hungry, footsore, and tired; besides which we had not the slightest idea where to get a lodging or anything to eat. Passing the end of a lane in a very lonesome part, I saw a ladder which seemed to lead to the loft of a stable, so, as there was no house or any human being in view, we decided to explore this loft; and here, sure enough, we found, among the hay and straw, very comfortable quarters, our only fear being that the farmer or his man would be coming early in the morning before we had slept off our dreadful weariness. That, however, did not happen; we awoke at daybreak, and attempted to leave the loft by the way we had come in. Our consternation may be imagined when we found we were locked in. We could find no lock, latch, or bolt, on the inner side of the stout door, nor could we, with our united strength, make it yield the eighth of an inch. Of course we concluded the farmer had been there before we awoke, and discovering us, had securely locked us in whilst he went for the constable. Failing to make an exit by the way we had entered we began a minute examination of the large loft. At one end of the room

we discovered a trapdoor, which, on lifting, we saw
was immediately over the manger of a couple of wagon
horses, evidently waiting breakfast. We saw there was
a door leading into a field, but we fancied it would be
locked; then the drop from the loft was a long one for
small boys, and we were rather afraid the horses might
resent the intrusion. So we decided to further explore
our prison before we attempted it. Fortunately we came
across another trapdoor at the other end of the loft, and
this we found looked down on a granary partitioned into
compartments for the various kinds of corn and other
food for horses and cattle. The compartment immediately under the trapdoor was nearly full of beans, so, as
we could be no worse off there than in the loft, we decided
to drop into the beans, and take the chance of finding
the door unlocked. To our delight it was so, and, with
our pockets filled with beans and corn, we were quickly
on the highway once more. Before we passed away
from the stable, I took a last look at the outside of the
loft with that awful door, and at once saw what had
given us half an hour's misery and suspense; it was provided with a huge wooden latch, on the outside only,
which, when we closed the door, securely imprisoned us.

We had not gone far on this day's tramp when the
mutiny broke out afresh. We had yet, perhaps, thirty
miles to go before we should reach our goal. Whining
and crying all the time, the small boy declared he could
walk no farther, although he was quite ready to face
the long walk back; and, what was worse, the big boy,

who had been showing signals of distress all the previous day, was almost as bad. I alone was eager to be going forward; I must, however, confess that the dread of what was in store for me, as the result of the summons, may have had something to do with it; but the main reason, I do believe, was my intense desire to see this miraculous London, and find my way to the fame and glory which I firmly believed should one day be mine; and only one thing softened me in the least, that was the thought of my mother. I did not want to go back, and I did not like going on by myself, so after vainly appealing to them in language the most forceful I could command, a happy thought struck me; we would draw straws for it, and which ever drew the longest should decide; I knew the odds were two to one against me, but I made them swear to abide by this chance. Fate was against me; the small boy drew the long straw, for which I very unjustly gave him a smart blow with my stick. We turned homeward again, and how we managed the three days' weary—and to me—hopeless tramp I don't know. When we reached the outskirts of Birmingham we were all in a pitiable condition; dirty, hungry, and ragged; my poor boots quite gone, and my feet blistered. We reached the Stratford Road—perhaps two miles from the centre of the town—about mid-day. My companions decided to go on at once to their homes on the opposite side of the town. I would not face this ordeal; ashamed of my condition I lay under a hedge in one of the fields till it was nearly dark, then crept out, and very slowly,

with pain in every step, made my way in the same direction. Half way up the Bull Ring I heard a voice shout,
" There he is," and looking up, I saw my father and an
elder brother. It appears that when they returned from
their work, they had heard from my companions where
they had left me, and they were searching for me. When
I reached home my poor mother shed tears of joy, and
all the family seemed glad to see the wanderer's return,
and, after all, the punishment for this escapade was not
what I had anticipated and perhaps deserved. Of course
I had to appear before the magistrate, who happened to
be on that occasion a humane and sensible man, who after
hearing all that Mr. John had to say against me, put a
few questions to me as to my reasons for running away.
My answers seemed to impress him favourably, so with
a mild caution not to do it again, he dismissed me ; and
I know I took away an impression that he spoke much
more harshly to Mr. John than to myself.

CHAPTER III

Boys' games and fights—How the Alderman stopped a fight—
The death of the Iron Duke, and what I thought of him—
A daring burglary—Early gaming—" Going over " at the
theatre—Another runaway to London—I visit Westminster
Abbey and House of Commons—A prodigal returned—
Two months in gaol—A ride with Kossuth

In looking back to these early days of my apprenticeship
I am struck with the great change which has taken place
in the character and disposition of the lads of the working
classes, especially in regard to their sports and pastimes.
In these twentieth century days opportunities and encouragement for out-of-door sports are afforded to the very
poorest, such as were unknown to the like in my young
days.   Proper playgrounds are provided ; in many places
extensive, and made beautiful with trees and shrubs and
flowers, and kept like any nobleman's grounds, and all
at the public expense.   Football, cricket, lawn-tennis, and
other healthy games, each in its season, are freely
provided.   Public baths, where they may learn to swim,
at a nominal charge, and schools where they may get an
excellent education for nothing.   In these days there are
not only the Saturday afternoons, but Bank Holidays,
and lots of other holidays during the year.   I, as a very
young lad, had to begin to work at eight o'clock Monday

morning, and, with one hour for dinner, worked till
seven o'clock at night—and this every day in the week,
and frequently, in busy times, we worked twelve or
fourteen hours for the day instead of ten.   My only bath
was in the by no means perfectly pure water of the canal
quite near to Snow Hill, then perhaps the busiest
thoroughfare in Birmingham, and it was there, when quite
a child, I learnt to swim.   What would the genteel youth of
these days say to that ?   During my apprenticeship my
only playground was the public street.   Hundreds of
times, I and a gang of lads have played " pitch back,"
" fox and dowdy," " bear and tender," and other rough
games in the middle of the roadway at the junction of
Constitution Hill and Livery Street, a spot now crowded
with electric tramway cars, cabs and vehicles of all sorts
—with scores of people—the policeman among them—
looking on.   These comparatively innocent games were
often diversified by street fights ; that is one set of lads
would make a raid on those of another locality, often with
quite serious results.   I suppose there never were such
inveterate fighters as the Birmingham lads of those days.
Among my fellow-apprentices there was one rule never
broken, every newcomer had to be " put through the mill "
as it was called ; which means that he was pitted against
one of the other lads, of like age and size, and they had
to prove, by fistic prowess, which was the better man of
the two ; and the spot where these battles usually took
place was in the path through St. Paul's Churchyard,
close to the door of that church, where there happened to

be a nice even bit of ground.   There I have done battle
myself, and there seen many battles fought.   It is amazing
how vividly some of these old boy fights, of more than
sixty years ago, come back to my memory.   I remember
so well how an amiable little gentleman, on his way
from his home—I think—in Vyse Street, to his business
in Great Charles Street, would frequently stop these fights
and lecture us on the folly and wickedness of our conduct,
and I can recall his grave and sonorous voice, with his
gentle pleading manner.   After these times he became a
town councillor, an alderman, a magistrate, and, for
many long years, one of the most honoured of Birmingham's public men—his name was Henry Manton.   Somehow his gentleness cowed me a good deal, and I never could
offer him the rudeness which occasionally he received for
his well-intentioned interference.   I recall a time I was
doing battle with a lad in Ludgate Hill when I caught
sight of the little gentleman walking sharply towards us—
and by his side a small well-dressed boy with a large white
tippet collar on.   The sight of him, without a word, was
enough to knock all the fight out of me, and I really think
that was about one of my last battles of this kind, for on
this occasion he lectured me till I was ashamed of myself.
In after years I came to be well acquainted with Henry
Manton, revering and respecting him.   I have sometimes
wondered whether the small school boy with the white
collar remembers this incident—he, too, has been for
many years an honoured and prominent public man in
Birmingham and, like his father, grown old and grey in

her service; and, quite recently, has been honoured by King George with a knighthood.

By the time I had arrived at the mature age of fifteen I was a really good reader and was discarding the trash of former days for purer and nobler literature, poetry being my chief delight. Burns, Byron, Oliver Goldsmith and Pope were my saints; Shakespeare was my God. The others I read with intense pleasure, committing to memory many of their gems; Shakespeare I worshipped, and there were few of the great speeches and soliloquies in his most popular plays I could not repeat from memory.

Shabby little editions of separate plays were published at a very low figure, and all these, one after another, I managed to buy, and very largely committed their contents to memory while I was busy with my work; of course I had to conceal them expeditiously when " Mr. John " was paying us one of his flying visits. To do this I had invented a rather ingenious substitute for a " tool rack," which usually was simply a piece of flat wood on legs, something like a small stool; in the top of the stool holes of various sizes were cut, and in these the drills and other tools in constant use were placed—ready to the hand. My invention, for the same purpose, was merely a box without a lid, turned upside down, so all I had to do, when danger was scented, was to lift the box and push the book under it. This contrivance was undetected and useful to me for several years, and I never scrupled about using it, and I don't believe I should have done so had I been possessed of a much more tender conscience than I could honestly claim, because I was at this time a sort of piece worker—that is my day's work was set me, and it had to be done before I could leave the place. So, while I filed and chiselled and drilled, I had ever the beloved little volume before me, and was committing its choicest bits to memory. And I not only read a good deal during my work, I composed any quantity of doggerel verse which I am quite sure I believed to be real poetry.

I remember when some one brought to the shop the news of Wellington's death, how I broke out with an impromptu poem in three verses while I was engaged in the hardening and tempering of my steel drills, and that, I suppose, supplied the figure used in the first verse ; what the other verses were like I quite forget. One verse, however, will be enough to show how I regarded the great warrior, for we were then too near the Reform Meetings on Nerhall Hill for Birmingham people to forget in what way the Duke had threatened to cure the old town's radical behaviour. Well, here's the first verse. I wish I could recall the other two, which I have no doubt whatever were equally bad—

> The Iron Duke is dead—cruel and brave—
> His hard steel heart death shall anneal,
> And he whose word filled fat many a grave
> Now makes the grave a meal.

The reader must not imagine that all this reading and writing had made me altogether a changed character. I read and wrote because I could not help it, and

I did many worse things, I suppose, for the same reason.

The warfare with Mr. John and his father had not abated in the least ; rather, I think, it had grown more fierce with my growth ; and looking back to some of the dreadful things we did I feel half inclined to distrust my memory, and put them down to the exuberant imagination of a romantic lad. Alas ! it is all too true, and how often have I longed—not only to forget these things—but to wipe them clean out of the book of my life. I am about to tell the true story of what the newspapers of sixty years ago called " A Daring Attempted Burglary " ; and in their description of the affair they very grossly libelled the Birmingham gentlemen of the burgling profession, because, in the first place, they described what a bungling attempt it was, and secondly because the professional gentlemen had nothing whatever to do with it. I know, but I won't say, who planned the burglary, but I will tell who attempted to carry out the plan.

The desire to free themselves from this bondage of apprenticeship was very strong with all the lads—with myself, and three or four working with me, it had become an intense passion. We knew that the instruments which held us down were pieces of paper called " Indentures " : these we also knew were kept in a small safe in the office, and we believed that could we possess ourselves of these bits of paper we should be free. Believing " the end justified the means " we determined to get them. There were four of us in it. One lad volunteered to hide himself in the works at closing time, and, at midnight, unbolt the door at the back, and admit his fellow-desperadoes. Then we were to borrow a truss or two of Mr. Jennings' hay—Mr. Jennings being the milkman who housed his cows most conveniently for our purpose, in a shed quite close to the door where we intended to make egress with the safe. The hay was to be laid thickly across the yard of the works, so that when we rolled the safe over it the sound would be muffled, and nobody disturbed. Then we were to hide ourselves and the safe in the cowshed until we heard the policeman pass that part of his " *beat*." One of the lads would now be told off to borrow a strong handcart belonging to a cooper near by, and which we knew was always to be found in the cooper's badly fenced little yard. Thereafter all was plain sailing. We had only to wheel the iron box, which contained our indentures, down to one of the pools and tip it in, and we were all free. And this beautiful plan was carried out to the letter until we came to the borrowing of the handcart ; that was not to be found in the little back yard of the cooperage, or elsewhere ; nor any other thing helpful to us in this awful dilemma. It appears the handcart had been borrowed by somebody else the previous day, and not returned in time for our purpose. So, after vowing to be true to each other, and never tell what we knew of the burglary, we left the safe in the cowshed, and went home. The police theory of the matter was, as usual, ingenious, and generally accepted. No article of any kind having been stolen, excepting the safe, and that not having been tampered

D

with, it was clear the thieves had been disturbed early in their operations, and had fled, but not, as is usual in these cases, leaving any of their tools behind them.

The gambling habit was common among all our apprentices, and to having been so early inoculated with this fearful disease, and trained in its practice, must I attribute many of the evils of my after life; and I must confess the habit has clung to me through almost all the rough roads I have travelled. The odds and ends of boxwood and ivory in which we worked were ready to hand, and this very fact seemed to offer a temptation to manufacture dice and other implements of gaming; and we not only made them for constant use among ourselves, but we did quite a trade in them among the gamblers elsewhere; and I remember one of the lads, whose father was a professional gambler, was able to supply him with some very useful tools in the shape of loaded dice. This was done by inserting, immediately under the lowest number, a piece of lead, which, of course, gave the dice a tendency to fall with the high number topmost, or *vice versa*.

The money obtained by this early manufacturing on our own account was generally spent on sixpenny seats in the gallery of the old Theatre Royal, and as we were seldom able to get there until a large crowd had assembled at the doors, we adopted a method for securing seats in the front row which was common enough in those days, and known to galleryites as " *going over*." Just before the doors were opened, one of the lads would hoist another on to the top of his shoulders, and from there he would jump on to the top of the densely packed mass. and so reaching the doors he would wedge himself down in front of the first comers. This practice occasionally led to difficulties with the police, and sometimes to a rough handling by the sufferers.

Once I was near neighbour to a big fellow who had misjudged the time for " going over," so when he arrived at the doors and began wedging himself down they were suddenly thrown open and he fell into the passage on his back, and was badly hurt by the people trampling over him.

The previous year's abortive attempt to become a hero had in nowise quenched my ambition in this direction, and my yearning for freedom and hatred of my trade and environment were stronger than ever. Oh, how I longed to be in London, where I was quite sure I should be able to do something wonderful. My day dreams were beautiful, and the castles I built in the air marvellous creations. So it does not seem strange, my brain crowded as it was with romantic ideas, that I should again run away and try to realise my beautiful day dreams. I loved the country, and missed none of the very few opportunities I had for long rambles far away from the purgatory of my workshop.

One morning I left home with the intention of going to work. A strict rule was that you must be there at eight o'clock. I was one minute late, and found myself " locked out " for a quarter of a day. I was exasperated, so determined I would make a full day's holiday of it and risk the consequences. I went for a long walk up the London Road. I declare that when I started I fully intended to return home the same night; the sun shone warm and bright, and the country, in all the beauty of its autumnal tints, was simply glorious; and I walked on and on. It happened that about what time I should have turned homeward I fell in with some tramps going to London. The temptation was too strong for me; I had very little money about me, but I never turned back, and three or four days later—again footsore and hungry— I found myself in London. I did not find any of the streets paved with gold, but, unfortunately, as it turned out, I found my way to the lodging of an elder brother somewhere in the neighbourhood of St. Luke's. After good feeding and a night's rest I was all right, and felt I ought to see some of the wonderful places I had read of before I proceeded on my quest of glory.

The very first place I made for was Westminster Abbey, and I shall never forget the overpowering sensation of reverence which possessed me as I entered its walls at Poets' Corner; I not only bared my head, but I felt that I ought to take off my shabby boots. I spent most of the day there and about the Houses of Parliament and the river.

Towards evening I hung about the entrance to the House of Commons for a long time, trying to screw up courage to enter; I did so want to hear the wonderful orators I had read about. At last I managed it. I was in one of the lobbies, where I saw a lot of quite ordinary-looking mortals—mostly hatless—hurrying and scurrying about with no apparent purpose. I ventured to ask a looker on like myself who the gentlemen were. He was good enough to tell me they were members, and even to point some of them out by name. A bluff elderly man with a wealth of whisker and curly hair he called " old Pam," and the undersized rather shabby little fellow with him was Lord John Russell. He was also good enough to tell me I could hear some of these wonders of eloquence if I got an introduction from a member. " Did I know one ? " I don't think I could have professed any intimate acquaintance with our member, George Frederick Muntz, but I am sure I told him I knew him very well by sight, and that was perfectly true, because I had seen him scores of times with his enormous whiskers and immense stick, which he always carried, pass down Constitution Hill on the way from his house at Hockley, to his rolling mills in Water Street. The upshot of it was that I introduced myself to our member, who, after asking me a few questions, kindly placed me in the Strangers' Gallery, where, I regret to say, my first disillusionment, regarding London, took place. I have no idea what was the subject of the debate, but I know I came away quite disgusted ; not one of the speakers, in strength of lung and power of eloquence, approached Arthur O'Neil and other Chartist leaders I had heard hold forth in a little chapel, somewhere near the top of Livery Street in Birmingham. I met with several other disillusionments during the three or four days I was sight-seeing in London ; then came, without the slightest warning, the end—for the present—

of all my dreams of glory. My elder brother was an extremely prosaic individual, without a particle of my romantic nature, or appreciation of the noble impulses which had brought me to London. One morning he awoke me very early, it seemed to me in the middle of the night ; after giving me some breakfast he bade me follow him, he did not say whither. After a long trudge through the streets I found myself in a great railway station. I was placed in charge of the guard of a train leaving at six o'clock—the parliamentary train, the only cheap means of travelling during the day. In those times only first and second-class passengers were cared for. I was placed with a couple of men who were travelling to Birmingham, and who promised my brother they would see I got back there. So stowed away in a sort of cattle truck, stopping at every little station on the way, and at some of them shunted for a considerable time while the swells went by, I arrived at what is now the goods station in Curzon Street. What a change has taken place since those days ; now I frequently take my place in quite a luxurious third-class carriage of a corridor train, and am whisked down to Birmingham in a couple of hours.

My reception at home was very like what it had been on the previous occasion ; my dear mother wept tears of joy, kissing and clinging to me as though she had recovered the most blessed thing life held for her, instead of a disreputable young scamp who deserved to be horse-whipped.

The sequel to my latest escapade was a serious affair ;

not again was I to escape so lightly. A summons had been issued, followed, on my non-appearance, by a warrant. My mother, on her knees, pleaded for mercy. Mr. John and his father were obdurate; they would have their pound of flesh. The warrant was in the hands of one of the cleverest policemen; they would have me captured, and, if possible, sent to prison. My poor mother came home broken-hearted, and told me there was no mercy for me. But for her I would have run away again, but I could not leave her. Quite early in the morning, the day after my mother's unavailing intercession for me, the clever policeman put in an appearance at my home; it happened, at that moment, I was in the cellar under our living room getting a bucket of coal for my mother. I heard her scream and guessed the reason; then I heard her sob, " Come up, my lad, the policeman has come for you." " Tell him to wait a bit," I replied. He didn't wait long, but it was a little too long; so that when he went down the cellar to fetch me he found the small iron door through which the coal was shot into the cellar, wide open, and the bird flown; and by one device or another I contrived to keep my freedom for nearly a week, and then I gave myself up, my mother, fearful of my running away again, begging me to do so. I was brought before a magistrate, less humane than the one who tried me before, and was sent to prison for two months. I was confined in that very gaol so soon to be made notorious by the infamous cruelties of that wretch Austin, the Deputy-Governor, and which made copy for Charles Reade's great novel, *Never too Late to Mend*; and I can never forget the kind-hearted old Governor, Captain Machonicie, asking, " What dreadful crime can a little lad like this have committed to deserve such a sentence." Nor when the answer came, how he laid his hand gently on my head, murmuring, " Poor boy—poor boy." I was condemned to two months' solitary confinement, and it seemed two years. Every day I was longing for the sight of one dear face, many a time I stood on the top of my stool where I could just get a glimpse of the lane in front of the gaol, and see, now and then, a passenger go by, always praying she would some day come by and look up to me. Once I got sight of a woman I knew ; she kept a small milkshop at the Sand Pits, and her son was a fellow-apprentice. She came to a farm near the gaol for her daily supply, which she carried in cans suspended from the old-fashioned " yokes " on her shoulders. The sight even of this poor woman gave me some pleasure, but, oh ! how I yearned for the sight of my own mother. I don't think I ever had realised, up to this time, how much I loved her. In my old age I am certain of one thing, and this has been the one abiding faith of my whole life, this damnable apprenticeship and what came of it, so incensed me and soured my nature, that, but for her great love for me and my love for her, I should have been a much worse lad and a much worse man.

While I was in prison the only books I was allowed were the Bible and a hymn book. Both I read through more than once, and many of the hymns I committed to memory, and when I returned to my hated work I read more than ever, no longer confining myself to poetry. I read history, biography, novels and political works, taking an especial delight in the politics of those revolutionary times, and such an out and out young Birmingham Radical was I, that when Kossuth came to Birmingham I met the procession at its entrance to the borough, and it must have been at some risk that I ran among the horses and carriages, until I secured a seat on the back axle of the very carriage the great man himself was seated in. And so I rode through Deritend, Digbeth and New Street to the top of Broad Street, and more than once, when Kossuth stood up to bow his acknowledgments to the enormous masses which lined the whole route, cheering him with wildest enthusiasm— as he rested his hand on the back of the carriage, I, more madly enthusiastic than my elders, managed to touch his hand, and that touch thrilled me as if it had been the touch of a god, and several times his kindly eyes met mine, looking down at me with a smile.

CHAPTER IV

A new friend and a Sunday school—Early literary efforts—
My mechanical invention and what " Mr. John " did with
it—My first meeting with the Rev. Charles Vince—I am
tempted to become a parson—Poetry and love—I once more
run away and become an actor—Am liberated from my
apprenticeship and perfect my invention—I become a manufacturing jeweller—Married—I am a newspaper proprietor,
editor and general manager—A useful deal with George
Cadbury

WHEN about seventeen years old I became acquainted
with a youth who was to influence my life, very strangely
for a number of years, aye, probably, for all the future
of my checkered and strenuous career. He induced
me to join him at a Sunday school at Mount Zion,
Birmingham.

A wild, boyish Bohemian, with dangerous tendencies,
I found here something appealing to another side of my
nature. I became a member of educational classes,
mental improvement societies, literary and debating
clubs, and in the latter, especially, I soon took quite a
prominent place.

At one of the latter societies I frequently met a young
man then preparing himself, at a big, square, ugly old
house, on Spring Hill, to become a Congregationalist

preacher. Quite a striking figure among us was this intellectual, dark-skinned, and somewhat sombre-looking young man, who, by and bye, shall become a sort of curate to the famous John Angel James, then succeed him, and thereafter almost eclipse him in the matter of fame, and become a great power, politically and otherwise, in Birmingham, and known through the length and breadth of the land as Dr. R. W. Dale.

Long before these days, indeed almost as long as I could remember, I had been in the habit of writing verses, and now, as I have said, I fancied myself quite a poet. I was encouraged in this conceit, I believe, by the fact that almost every effusion which I sent to Sunday school magazines was accepted and printed ; and sometimes the men who presided over these periodicals wrote me nice little letters of encouragement, some of which I have preserved to this day, and am even weak enough to cherish them. One of these, I remember, was from Mr. Edward Baines (afterwards Sir Edward), editor and proprietor of the *Leeds Mercury*, and sometime M.P. for that great city. He was also editor of *The Appeal*, a religious little weekly, to which I had contributed my verse, and in a nice letter, before me as I write, he assures me that if only I will be a good boy I shall, some day, write something well worth printing : alas ! alas ! I suppose I was not a good boy.

I was now reading more eagerly than ever Chaucer, Spenser, Shakespeare and Milton. I read so constantly in the streets, as I went to and fro between my home and

my purgatory of a workshop, that people called me the
" reading lad."

But let it not be supposed that I detested my trade a
whit the less since I had been reclaimed from my wilder
ways. I now felt, I do believe, more keenly than ever
the galling of the chain that bound me, although I had
more control of myself, and was no longer in the habit of
expressing my abhorrence in the same powerful language.

As testifying to this I must relate an incident of those
days which intensified my hatred of this bondage. I
was beginning to vary my reading and writing by the
exercise of an inventive faculty. I had an idea that
an immense amount of labour might be saved in a certain
part of the manufacture of rules by the application of
machinery driven by steam power, where small circular
saws and circular cutters, guided by one man, could be
made to do the work of chisels and files and saws in
twenty hands.

To realise this idea I set about making a little model
of a machine out of bits of waste boxwood.   I had thought
it out and worked at it for a month or two during every
minute of the time I could spare ; hiding my model, during its progress toward completion, in the cunningly
contrived tool rack already described.

It was nearing completion, and I was sanguine of its
success, as events, a few years later, proved I had a right
to be, when arriving at my work one morning I found my
beautiful machine on my " bench " smashed into little bits,
and amid the ruins a cheap little copy of " Hamlet," also

torn into pieces.   This I knew was the work of " Master John," and it aroused all the devil that was in me, the which had been for some time dormant.   I raved and swore like my old self, threatening vengeance of the direst sort on my enemy, forgetting, for the moment, all the lessons I had been learning at Mount Zion.   However, I did nothing terrible, but, cooling down, sensibly decided to bide my time and go on with my inventions when better opportunities should come, which, after a time, as we shall see, they did.

I shall now relate a little incident which befell me in these days, and one which was to influence a good deal of my after life ; and in my old age I am apt to think it might have been better for me if I had allowed it to have influenced my life all through.   The incident may have little interest for many of my readers, but to some Midlanders, and old Birmingham men particularly, I am sure it will be interesting.

I was going home to my dinner, my dirty apron rolled round me, and tucked up at the waist, with a book in my hand as usual, had just reached Mount Street, when I literally ran against a ruddy, round-faced, boyish-looking young man dressed in a country-made suit of black, with the regulation parsonic " white choker " round his neck.   He was bigger, and a few years older than myself, and had, I thought, rather a clumsy gait with him.   After the collision I looked up into his face ; and what a face it was !   I remember it—after all these years—as I remember the face of my mother.   A broad, beaming, genial—aye, even jovial—sort of face, and set in it a pair of eyes full of the fire of genius and kindly human nature, and they captivated me from the moment I saw them. I fancy he rather liked my looks, too, for instead of rating me for carelessness, which he might have done, he laughed good-humouredly, chatting pleasantly as we walked up the street together.

" Can you tell me," he asked, " where I shall find Mount Zion Chapel ? "

" Oh, yes. I am going past it, and will show you the way," I replied.

Of course, it soon came out that I attended the Sunday school there. This appeared to please him, and he volunteered sundry pieces of information about himself which made it clear he was, at that time, a student of Stepney College, a total stranger to Birmingham, not knowing a soul in the place. Also that he had received an invitation from the good folk at Mount Zion to preach a trial sermon.

" So you will, perhaps, hear me to-morrow," he said, " and, if the people like me, I may come to be your minister. If that happens I would like to know you better, and perhaps I may be of some service to you."

And then he made me promise, should these hopes of his as to the pastorship come to anything, that I would visit him.

Well, I heard him preach next day to a company of poor people who had been struggling for several years to keep the place going, while loaded with debt and a weekly dwindling congregation. His success was instant and magnetic, and he was thereupon invited to become our pastor ; and although he had not finished his time at Stepney, almost at once entered upon his duties. I kept my promise, and we became great friends ; and many an hour, after my work was done at night, and frequently before I went to it in the early morning, have I spent with him at his lodgings while he tried to cram me with Latin and other things, which he thought—good soul—would be needful in the future he was shaping for me ; this was loving and strenuous enough, but, alas ! doomed to futility. The rough granite this good man chiselled at—trying to polish—was obdurate, unworkable, and utterly impossible of being wrought into the well-meaning minister's ideal.

Well, this comely, country-bred young parson, who, a few years before, was himself a hard-working carpenter lad, was Charles Vince, who in due course became one of the most brilliant preachers in England ; not only an ornament and a glory to his own sect, but known and revered by all classes and creeds among whom he lived. A power in educational, social and political work, he finished his public life where he had begun it ; and when he died—which is a good many years ago—all Birmingham mourned for him ; the best of its citizens and many thousands of its toilers followed him sorrowfully to the grave. The jangle of sects and parties, for a day, was silenced. Roman Catholicism, Church of Englandism, Dissent, Atheism, Nothingarianism, and all the other isms and schisms stood by his grave, knowing that a good man and true had passed from their midst.

As for me, many years agone we had come to the parting of the ways, and thenceforth I had seen but little of him. He had won an eminent place in the world. I was one of its hardened sinners, and, shocking to relate, a professional betting man. Nevertheless, I left my business in the midst of it, that I might stand once more, and for the last time, beside my old friend and master; and I feel no shame to say that many bitter tears burnt my face, and many a bitter thought tortured me, as I watched them hide for ever from my view all that remained of one of the sweetest and noblest men I have ever known.

While I had lived under the influence of this wise and good man, not only had my whole character and conduct changed, but I had acquired much solid good in the way of education. His interest in me grew as we became more intimate, and his efforts to help me in the matter of education were most earnest; and, while he was a single man, he gave a good deal of time to this labour of love. I rather think there was a kind of conspiracy between the good man and two or three of the principal members of his congregation to make a parson of me, for the reason, I suppose, that I had shown some aptitude for public speaking. Mr. Thomas Adams, the timber merchant, Mr. McEvoy, and Mr. William Morgan, a well-known solicitor, and once town clerk of Birmingham, were, I had reason to believe, the chief conspirators, and each had occasionally hinted something of the kind: hence I was not surprised on receiving an invitation to call on Mr. Morgan at his offices in Waterloo Street, to get a proposal that I should be sent to college and prepared for the ministry. I think my old friend was hugely disappointed, and perhaps annoyed, when I was obliged to refuse this generous offer. My ambitions did not lead in this direction. I longed to go to college and get an education, the lack of which I began to feel so keenly. I knew myself better than they knew me, and I realised a danger they could not imagine, and I frankly confess I have never regretted my refusal to be made a minister.

The course I took did not rob me of the friendship of these gentlemen, or of Mr. Vince. I continued my membership of their congregation; every year becoming more active in the work of its various associations. I remember that I supplied the young ladies of the congregation for some time with a poem every month, which they printed and sold for the benefit of missions, or something of the sort. This brought me a good deal among the girls, which I do not think was good for me.

About this time there appeared in the Midlands an escaped American slave who made Birmingham his headquarters for a considerable time; and Mount Zion being the scene of many of his meetings I became intimate with him. His name was James Watkins, and although he had not the slightest education such was his natural eloquence, when he told of the horrors he had suffered as a slave and as a fugitive from slavery, that when I heard him for the first time he worked me into such a frenzy that

E

I went home and wrote some verses which I showed him the following day. These he had printed and sold them thereafter at all his lectures. Similar verses followed; and, as he sold very many of them, there is no doubt they were useful to him, and it is quite certain they caused him to propose a project which was even more useful. This was that he should tell me the story of his early days—his years of slavery, and his romantic escape : and that I should write *The Autobiography of a Fugitive Slave*, by James Watkins ; he promising to give me half the profits of the little booklet. I wrote every word of it, but he published it as an autobiography, and sold many thousands at sixpence each ; but I was never able to get a penny of the profits ; he was always going to pay me next week, but next week never came.

In these days, my brother and I with my early friend William Cook promoted a series of musical entertainments or, as the advertisements had it, " Great Juvenile Demonstrations," in the Birmi̲ ̲ ̲ ̲wn Hall. Cook, about whom I have much to say later on, was destined to occupy a big place in the public life of the town ; then, however, he was a very young man ; poor, but steady and respectable, and it was his tiny brother-in-law Teddie Scambler —" the Little Blind Boy "—apparently not more than six or seven years old—who was the great attraction at these entertainments, for nature had given him a marvellous voice, which filled the great hall with sounds as sweet as any I have heard.

The programme for the first of these demonstrations

provided for three short speeches from three young men ; and I was among the three selected. John Skirrow Wright, sometime M.P. I think for Nottingham—was chairman, but with voice strong as a lion's he failed to make himself heard. The youngsters wanted no speeches, they only wanted to hear Teddie and the music. My turn to speak came last ; the other two young men had tried to be heard, but had given it up as a bad job. Of course where the mighty voice of the chairman failed, these young untrained voices were not likely to succeed.

I thought I saw where the difficulty lay. Strength of voice or what a man had to say was nothing to do with it. It was entirely a question of getting a moment's quiet between the songs ; and I believed that might be possible by means of a little ruse. When my turn came the chairman said I had better not make my effort. This advice I politely refused to accept. " I have sent my brother," I said, " right to the top of the great gallery, so he may tell me whether I am heard there ; and I think I shall be heard, sir." Mr. Wright laughed, but he called upon me. Now came my ruse. Instead of attempting a feeble speech, trying to pierce the hubbub with my voice, I rushed to the front of the great platform and struck a horribly tragic attitude, pointing to the top of the great gallery. This was something new to them ; they all turned their heads towards what I pointed at ; and, in a moment, the silence was perfect. Then I began in my ordinary voice, which was audible all over the vast meeting of several thousand children—" There's a boy at the top of that gallery to whom I'm going to tell a story"; and they gave me rapt attention while I told them the thrilling story of "The Girl Martyr."

At this time there was employed at our works, but not in my workshop, a very clever woman about old enough to be my mother who was destined to be a disturbing force in my life. She was an intimate friend, a near neighbour, and, if I remember rightly, a relative of George Jacob Holyoake, under whose teaching she had become an avowed infidel. This woman took a strong fancy to me, and her cleverness and gift of argument attracted me to her. We had frequent bouts of reasoning, and, while enjoying them, they generally left me with a feeling that I had come out badly beaten. I have said she was clever; she was, moreover, a great reader, and far better up in the arguments against religion than I was in those for it. I knew she was setting herself to undo what Mr. Vince and Mount Zion had done for me. She supplied me with the literature of her society; made me acquainted with Voltaire and Rousseau, and among English writers, with Locke, Hume, Tom Paine, and others. *The Age of Reason*, which I read in secret, did more to unsettle me than all the others. For a long time I was bewildered and unhappy. I wanted to know the truth, but I did not want to desert my friends and the congenial work at Mount Zion.

How well I remember one night, after all my family had gone to bed, when I had hours of terrible wrestling with these doubts, in deep anguish, crying for light and guidance, and but little light came—just a glimmer from a thought that perhaps Mr. Vince might help me. Next day I went to him, telling him all my trouble and such help as he could give he gave me. Under his guidance, I began a course of reading which was to be the antidote to the poison. I think I read, in the first place, Simpson's *Plea for Religion*. Then one of Vince's favourite authors, Paley: *The View of Evidence, Natural Theology, Horæ Paulinæ*, and something of Lardner's. All this reading left me still unsettled; full of doubts and difficulties— pulled first one way and then another; so I went home one night, after a long debate with my friend the pastor, and burnt every book belonging to myself on both sides of the question; making a vow that I would read no more, and, if possible, think no more about it.

Seeking material for " copy " relating to my early life, I had recently occasion to " rummage " through an immense old oaken chest, which has been a cherished treasure from my boyhood, and which contains a marvellous assortment of odds and ends. Among them bundles upon bundles of letters neatly docketed and tied up with faded bits of ribbon, all in the handwriting of young girls, my various early sweethearts—half a score of them, at least. All gone ! Whither I know not. Some, doubtless, long since dead, others may have become wrinkled and disagreeable old grandmothers. Buried in this great chest, along with these early love-letters, are remnants of wool-worked slippers, worn-out worsted mittens, a few properties of amateur acting days, endless newspaper and magazine cuttings of my early poetic effusions—in those times I travailed a good deal in that line. Above these, and a heterogeneous mass of other things of more or less interest, is a layer of neat-looking gilt-edged little betting books, such as are used by young beginners. Alas, what a tale these would tell and what a sermon preach could they but talk. Among these I found an old empty envelope, bearing a northern postmark, not far from the famous city of York. The inside of the envelope was blurred and stained; on the outside—written with a pencil and still legible—were the following verses. Oh! what a dreadful bad time I must have been having.

A VIOLET

(Sent by Post)

Thou'rt welcome—welcome, lovely flow'r,
  With sweetly-scented breath,
Thou com'st to me in darksome hour,
And to my soul in sad, strange pow'r,
  Art preaching life and death.

Thou wert all fresh and fair and gay—
  A thing of beauty and grace—
When yestermorn the king of day
A trembling dewdrop kissed away
From thy heav'nward turning face.

And now, my flower, thy tiny head
  Hangs earthward evermore;
Charm of thy mystic life hath fled,
And thou art soiled and crushed and dead—
  Aye, dead! my bonnie flow'r!

E'en such is this poor life of ours.
  To-day, with flashing eye,
We stand erect as gaudy flow'rs,
Boasting of all our matchless powers,
  To-morrow we fade and die.

I insert these lines here to show the kind of thing I was writing in those days. Years after they were written they appeared in a Birmingham paper, and after that it ministered to my pride a little to see them copied into sundry other papers or periodicals.

'Twixt love and religion, I was pretty busy among the Muses while still in the " teens " of my years. These effusions brought me no money, but they did procure for me some considerable amount of local notice, especially among the young women folk, and I am afraid I fell in love, and out again, much too often. If any of my old sweethearts are still living, and remember these things against me, it will soften them something to know that looking back through all these years, a sad remorsefulness mingles with many pleasant memories associated with them. Youthful folly, and inconstancy, my dear old ladies, I frankly admit ; and, like poor Burns, I fall back on nature for an excuse. She gave me an ardent, impulsive temperament.

> " With passions wild and strong,
> And list'ning to their 'witching voice,
> Hath oft-times led me wrong."

I was continually, more or less, in a fever of love, and when about twenty I had a very severe attack. She was a charming little girl with kissable lips, rosy cheeks, and a merry pair of eyes. Her father's business took him to live in Sheffield, whither of course my Polly migrated. I was disconsolate, and flinging all my good resolutions, my books and classes, my religious pastors and masters, with the hard taskmaster, to whom I was bound, all to the winds, I followed her to Sheffield; and as I could not live entirely on love, became a member of one of the old-fashioned stock companies at the Theatre Royal, then under the management of poor old Charles Dillon.

I played sundry small parts for some months. Meanwhile, the course of true love was not running smoothly. I had, or fancied, a reason for jealousy, and walking through the darkness and drizzle from the theatre to my lodgings one certain midnight, I saw my figure reflected by the street lamps; strange thoughts flashed through my mind, leading to an instant revulsion of feeling.

" The shadow of an actor," I muttered; " to-night a sham nobleman in tawdry and unreal trappings; a thing of tinsel and make-believe; hollow and unreal—a veritable sham. Why not try to be, in some sort, a real nobleman— or, anyway, a man—a real live man with a purpose, and not a sham? "

Nature had given me eyes which had been of use to me, had shown me men, in the great town where I was born, who had lifted themselves out of poverty and obscurity into wealth and influence and high social position; apparently with brains of no better quality than my own. What these had done I would do—Why not? And more even.

Thenceforth the footlights flared on me no more for ever. Forests of painted lath, painted canvas oceans and mountains, with all the " props " and paraphernalia of the playhouse, from that moment were behind me. I would go back to Birmingham and face the consequences, which I knew might be serious. I acted on this resolution, and my reception was better than my deserts. At home, and among the good folk at Mount Zion, I was once again the prodigal son returned—a strayed sheep once more gathered to the fold. These good friends of mine—for friends they were, meaning me only good—not only interceded with my hard taskmaster that he should spare me the usual punishment of runaway apprentices— another term of imprisonment—but induced him to forego the remainder of the time which belonged to him, and cancel my indentures.

I was no sooner free than I set to work as only a free man can work, and with an energy which was a part of me at that time.

The opportunity I had longed for at length arrived. I started on another model of my invention, working night and day at it until it was completed, and then showed it to Mr. Thomas Bradburn, one of the largest rule makers in the town. He was so struck with it he engaged me at once, and from this model, with a little assistance from a practical machinist, I made the machine, which was perfectly successful, and which, steam driven, enabled me with its circular saws and bits of steel to do the work of ten men. I may say the invention was by no means welcomed by Mr. Bradburn's workmen, and as long as I remained in his employ I had to be carefully guarded, locked in a room by myself during the few hours it was necessary for me to work in each day.

Now, for the first time in my life, I was able to earn more than I wanted to spend ; and so it was not long before I had saved what I thought would launch me in business on my own account.

My intimate chum was a journeyman jeweller, whom I induced to leave his situation and join his skill and workmanship to my capital and aptitude for salesman and traveller. And so we started in a small way, but with high hopes, as manufacturing jewellers. Our reputation as steady young men who meant to go ahead was very helpful to us. My old employer, who had benefited by my inventions, discounted as many accommodation bills as I chose to take to him, out of the goodness of his heart, and at *the modest rate of 25 per cent. per annum.*

These early days of my business career were not only prosperous, but exceedingly happy ones, which I look back to as the happiest of my whole life. Business was so full of promise, and I so full of love for a meek-eyed young thing, the gentlest and truest human being I have ever known, I felt justified in getting married, and starting a home on my own account. The bustle of trade, and these tenderer matters, did not wholly divert attention from my literary purposes ; but I would get rich first, money was such a power—would get rich quickly, if possible, and make haste back to my early love—the sacred Muse.

Dr. F. R. Lees, of Leeds, originator, I believe, of the

Maine Law movement in England, an eminent lecturer, a powerful thinker, and a writer of great ability, had become known to me through some articles I had contributed to a north-country paper with which he was connected. I recall how, in those days, at his invitation, I spent a few days with him at his home at Meanwood, near Leeds. We sat up nearly all one night discussing these literary aspirations of mine, and my " unholy means " of attaining their fruition, for so he stigmatised my burning desire to be rich ; and yet he knew that no mere sordid love of wealth moved me ; knew that my aims were worthy ; but I can never forget how earnestly he pleaded with me that I would throw down this golden idol, whose worship would blur all my beautiful visions, harden my heart, stunt and enfeeble my intellect, and make impossible any return to the pursuit of my ideals. This, and a great deal more he said, placing before me, in powerful language, the worthiness and beauty of my own ideals ; and showing me how much nobler it were to fail in such pursuit than it would be to succeed by prostrating myself to this base god. I was a very young man, and thought I knew best what was good for myself. Alas ! how many times in recent years have I wished I had listened to the advice of wisdom and experience.

In connection with my early literary work, I may here claim that I originated the first halfpenny newspaper that I ever heard of, and possibly it was the very first that ever existed in England. It was named *The Banner*, and was very largely devoted to the interests of the temperance movement in Birmingham, reporting its meetings and advocating its claims. It was printed on good paper, neatly got up, and had, I think, a very respectable circulation for a local effort of this kind. I had associated with me at its commencement Mr. Fred Johnson, a Birmingham accountant. I, however, did the editing, most of the writing, reported the meetings, and even got the advertisements. After the death of Mr. Johnson, Mr. William White, an influential member of the Society of Friends, helped with the work, and his firm, White & Pike, printed the paper, and ultimately they took it over altogether.

It was in connection with this little paper that I made my next visit to London, somewhere between fifty and sixty years ago. I lodged at a none too clean little coffee-house in Holywell Street ; which in recent years has gone, with other of the old streets thereabout, to make way for Aldwych and the Kingsway. This house, if I remember rightly, was called Colliver's Temperance Hotel, and was the resort, indeed I may say the workshop, of a great number of the *penny-a-liners* who supplied the London newspapers with " copy," for which in these days each paper has its own staff of well trained and capable reporters. The coffee shop was divided into about a dozen little pens, each having a narrow little seat on either side of the table. Here I sat with these poor wretches day after day, for two or three weeks, scribbling my impressions of the scenes and characters I had met with in my night rambles among the waifs and strays of the great city, which appeared each week in *The Banner* as " Notes of a Visit to London," by Simon Quiz.

While on this subject I may say that *The Banner* was not the only newspaper which owed its birth to my initiative. A good many years after, and while deeply engrossed with my turf and other businesses, and in connection with Mr. " Barty " Weekes, a Birmingham solicitor, I made a more ambitious attempt in journalism, starting a penny weekly, devoted to general news. This venture cost me a good deal of money, no end of hard work and anxiety during the ten years we kept it afloat. But at that time I was a member of the Board of Guardians, the Balsall Heath Local Board and the King's Norton Rural Sanitary Authority, which two Boards governed a large district which is now in the city of Birmingham, and I found the *South Birmingham News* a very handy weapon, and useful to me in many ways while engaged in public life ; but I began to tire of the cost and work of it, especially as I had on my hands at the time a large manufacturing concern, employing nearly two hundred workpeople, besides a considerable betting business. And when on the point of giving it up I had the good fortune to come across a purchaser with a liberality and generosity I have never found equalled in business. This was Mr. George Cadbury, the present head of the great cocoa firm.

" Will you find out what the paper has cost you from the commencement ? " that gentlemen inquired during one of our interviews regarding its sale. I told him the amount at our next meeting. I thought of course he was about to base an offer for the paper on these figures, and that we might possibly see a small moiety of the money back again, especially as I was acquainted with Mr. Cadbury's reputation for generous dealings in business matters. Imagine my feelings when he quietly remarked,

"Oh, that's what the paper has cost you. Well, I wouldn't like to feel that anybody was losing by what I bought of them, so that's the amount I'll give you for the paper."

Mr. Cadbury afterwards spent a good deal of money on it, and it is to-day a prosperous journal, known as the *Birmingham News*.

I must now, however, hark back a few years, and tell of early business struggles, and fatal efforts to get rich quickly.

CHAPTER V

Some of Birmingham's successful men—The Tangyes—William
  Cook—Business struggles—I become commercial traveller—
  I am tempted and fall—An infallible system and its inventor
  —I go to Goodwood races—The infallible system in full
  swing—The system fails and I am ruined

DEAR old Birmingham is in many ways a wonderful
place, and from the nature and variety of her manufactures
offers opportunities for young men who mean to " get on "
unequalled by any other city in His Majesty's dominions.
Outside London there is, I suppose, no city where there
are so many prosperous, well-to-do-men, who have worked
their way up from " the bench."

Some of these I have known intimately, and in one way
and another have rubbed against many of them in my
time. Here is a story which will illustrate my meaning :

While I was busy on the inventions I have referred to,
I had occasion to get a matter of turning done, or something of the kind, so found my way down a poor court
in Mount Street where a number of young beginners of
various trades—too poor to have steam engines of their
own—rented small workshops, with the use of steam
power from somebody else. The two young engineers
I wanted to see, and whom I did see, in their greasy aprons

and work-a-day dress, bore the Cornish name of Tangye.

When my engineering business was done with these young men, I passed into another shop in the same court, where I found two other industrious young strugglers, one of them an intimate friend and the brother-in-law of my own partner, who were renting power for the purpose of pointing pins, and making small brass rivets, which should shortly supersede the old-fashioned cobbler's waxed thread, to secure the soles to the " uppers " of our boots and shoes. The two young engineers became millionaires, patrons of art, munificent endowers of hospitals, art galleries, and schools ; founders and heads of one of the great engineering concerns of the world.

The other two young strugglers founded and built up probably the largest pin works in the world ; one of them, William Cook, the brother-in-law of my partner, was for many years an alderman and magistrate of the city, and for a time M.P. for one of its divisions, and, I suppose, a very wealthy man when he died quite recently.

With this firm of Harrison & Cook I had intimate relations when both our young firms were struggling to keep their heads above water. I shall never forget the first time I entered the low, dirty little shop where they rented power of Mr. Pumphrey, a well-known Quaker manufacturer. Cornelius Harrison was grinding and pointing the brooch pins, or tongs, as they were called, to be sold among the makers of cheap jewellery. William Cook was tending their one solitary machine, and a very ingenious one it was, turning out shoe rivets automatically and with great speed, and requiring but the least bit of attention on the part of my friend Cook.

"My dear Will," says I, "you could attend to half a dozen machines like this, if you had them." "Of course I could," he replied, "but I shall soon earn enough to get another."

This conversation set me thinking, and, some time after, I mentioned the matter to Mr. Bradburn, who readily agreed to discount bills for these young men on the *easy* terms I have named if I would agree to endorse them. This I was glad to do, so other machines were quickly at work, and the young firm began to make headway rapidly. The only difficulty now was to induce Messrs. Winfield to trust them with sufficient brass wire to keep pace with the machines ; and this difficulty was got over in much the same way, and some of the early difficulties of our own bus:ness, helped by Harrison and Cook, were surmounted by the like methods. As they were dissatisfied with the prices they were getting from the Birmingham "middle man," I suggested they should let me take these samples with me on a westward journey I was going with my own wares. They jumped at the idea of going direct to the users of these rivets, the great boot and shoe manufacturers. So, armed with a letter from the teacher of our early Sunday morning class, that gentle Quaker, William White—I hied away to that great firm of Quaker shoemakers, Clarks, of Street, in Somersetshire, and there opened an account for them which grew, I

F

believe, in after days, to large dimensions. The same thing happened with some great Bristol firms in the same trade.

So William Cook and I were great friends and helpful to each other while I remained in what he called " *The right path*," but I think he never quite forgave me for departing from it.

Without any very brilliant natural gifts, but with sterling honesty of purpose, indomitable will, strong common-sense, and an immense power of work, he reached riches and honours and a high place in the reverence and esteem of all sorts of people in the great city of his adoption. The last time I saw him, not long before his death—when he was " Sir William "—he talked, as he always delighted to do, of the old times we had known together when very young men ; of Mount Zion and our Sunday mornings at Severn Street adult school, of the few holidays we were able to get in those days, mostly spent among the glorious scenery of Gloucestershire ; where, in a tiny cottage in the tiniest of villages—hidden in a hollow of Rodborough Hill—he was born. These pleasant reminiscences, on more than one occasion, ended with a word which stung me a good deal more than I showed at the time. " Ah ! Dyke, old man," he would say, " you do well to call yours a ' wasted life,' I *have* done something with my life, and *you*, what might you have done if only you had——" etc.

These examples of the rise of great firms, from small beginnings in Birmingham, were by no means rare ; I could name many others whose origin and history I have watched. And now I am to make sorrowful confessions how I came to miss my chance of being found among them.

Considering how small was the beginning, our business grew with amazing rapidity. I did the travelling, my ground extending southwards to Penzance, and northwards to Edinburgh. Manufacturing jewellers, as a rule, sold their goods to the factors; I decided to take a bolder course for my little firm by going direct to the shop-keepers. I was wonderfully successful, orders rolled in almost faster than we could execute them; with the result that in less than a couple of years we found ourselves considerable employers of workmen—the masters of a thriving trade. In our employ, as assistant traveller and confidential help, was my dear old friend William Collins; what his help did for us—in all sincerity and with the best intentions—will shortly appear.

One Monday morning never to be forgotten by me, Collins came to the works big with fate for the prosperous young firm, now busy, and starting on the new week well; preparing a " *melt* " which, when properly mixed, rolled, cut up, and manipulated will be a barrow load of *bright gold*—brooches, earrings, and other ornaments. The ingredients which were to produce this display were already in the crucible; a hundred golden sovereigns, fresh from the mint, a parcel of pure silver; and with these, I am obliged to confess, an amount of copper, something more than twice the weight of its co-constituents combined.

The whole, when properly fused, shall be known in Hounds-ditch and elsewhere as " bright gold," in contradistinc-tion to " coloured gold," or gold of any particular carat warranted by hall-mark.

At this moment entered Mr. Collins, claiming time for instant private talk on a matter of urgency.

" Fire away, Will, and let me hear quickly what's the matter," I said.

" Well, then, to begin with, I'm come to tell you I'm giving up my job with you."

" Oh, indeed ! and may I ask wherefore ? " inquired I, with a feeling of alarm, knowing it must be a serious matter which could have driven my old friend to such a course.

" Well, the fact of the matter is," began Collins, " I've found a better trade, and one I wish you would join me in."

And then he proceeded to unfold a scheme which had taken many months maturing ; a scheme for backing horses on unerring mathematical principles—in fact, he had already given the system a trial on the quiet—for bits of silver only, and even in this modest way had it been good enough to earn a certain sovereign or more weekly. It could be worked just as easily in fivers and tenners, or in hundreds even, with capital behind you, and so a fortune realised almost at once ; and our ambitious young jeweller might save himself the years of plodding toil, become rich quickly, and so, while still young, with all the vigour of youth, be enabled to devote himself to those aims and pursuits he was ever dreaming of. At first I struggled against temptation—even thrust it from me with some disdain. Now, while I did want to make a lot of money, and that quickly, I must do myself the justice to say these desires were founded on no mere sordid motives; so I thought there could be no great harm in looking into the thing and examining my tempter's evidence, because if there really was anything in it, would not the end justify the means, etc.? So racing calendars for several seasons past, with copious sheets of foolscap, were instantly produced by our friend Collins; and, after a couple of hours' closest scrutiny, I was obliged to confess there was something in it. The scheme was revealed to me so clearly infallible that I turned out of the melting pot the hundred bright sovereigns and handed them to my friend, so he might catch the train for a distant race meeting, where the infallible system should be put into actual practice.

During the four days following, the scheme was in full work in the hands of its author—for the present, however, only on modest dimensions. On Friday night our agent returned, bringing back with him the hundred pounds and some ten pounds profit, which should have been considerably more, only that the first favourite had been missed on two occasions, the second favourite being backed by mistake, which had thrown the machinery a little out of gear. But with practice should we not be able always to find the true favourite? The great thing was, the principle could not fail. You had only to back the

favourite in the first event for a given—rather small
sum ; if that lost, increasing your stake on a graduating
scale drawn out with mathematical precision, no matter
how many times you lose—having nerve enough to plank it
down—the first time a favourite wins you get it all
back, and a lot besides.   Indeed, so good did it appear
we decided to give it a trial the following week.   It was
" Glorious Goodwood," and now behold me accompanied
with my guide, philosopher, and friend, fairly launched
on the turf in the character of a new punter.   On the
first day no favourite won either of the first four races,
and on the fifth we had to pull out and plank down
a larger sum than I relished.   However, I did it manfully,
posting the clean notes into the hands of a gentleman who
was offering liberal odds.   " And now," says I, " let us
go on to the stand and see the race."   We had scarcely
reached the top of the stand when the horses were on the
way, and in less than two minutes we had the unspeakable
pleasure of seeing the gee-gee I had backed romp past the
post the easiest of winners, and you may be sure it was
not long before we descended gleefully to the ring to
receive the money, altogether £60 ; £40 being the winnings,
and the remainder my own stake.   But, alas ! the bright
little gentleman of liberal odds, with whom I had betted,
was nowhere to be found ; we made inquiries in every
direction, among all sorts of people, explaining the circumstances ; among others, to one of the officials, who told
us rather curtly he thought " we were precious green " ;
a gentleman standing near winked his eye, saying face-

tiously, " It's all right, my boys, you'll see him again some day." Another bluntly declared we had been " welshed," whatever that might mean ; anyway, we saw him no more that week. Some weeks after I saw and accosted a genteel little fellow named Manning, feeling prepared to swear this was the very man, so I demanded the £60. But he swore in choicest English and in a positive manner that he had never been to Goodwood in his life, so you see it could not have been he. However, to return to the ring at Goodwood. While being annoyed at this loss, I was delighted with the soundness of the infallible method, and acted on it during the remainder of the week, only exercising great circumspection as to the men I betted with. At the end of the week we returned home—in spite of the one untoward event—with my capital intact, and a considerable profit. The following week the system was in full operation again at Brighton and Lewes, with equally good results. So was it for several weeks. I now began to find it difficult to hide my light under a bushel —or otherwise. In fact I was followed about the ring and became known as the successful new punter. I had now no longer need to pull out the " ready." I had a weekly account, hence I began to try the system on a higher scale. Alas ! however infallible our systems, the best of men are, after all, really fallible. Again I made a serious blunder, mistaking the true first favourites, which resulted in a couple of losing weeks, wherein went all the previous winnings and much more. So we find ourselves arrived at the famous York meeting. Here it was decided to go in for still larger results, the method having proved itself faultless, and my bungling alone blamable for partial failure.   Well, this same York meeting must remain a very memorable one.   All the good things were beaten, and, in fact, not one first favourite got home during the four days.   Surely an unheard-of calamity, enough to smash up any—the most infallible—system.   My readers will be able to picture to themselves what this would mean to a backer of first favourites, on the gradually increasing—or getting back—system.   Need I say I found myself on Friday night an utterly ruined man.   Not all the bright gold brooches, earrings and other ornaments in our establishment, stock-in-trade, household effects, with all our worldly belongings, would have sufficed to settle with the bookies on the following Monday.   In the vulgar parlance of the turf, I was obliged to " take the knock."

This was an ignominious ending to my grand hope of getting quickly rich, and being so enabled to plant my foot firmly on the ladder of my ambitions without the tedious humdrum processes of trade, which seemed to mean so many years of precious time lost.

CHAPTER VI

The turf has broken me and shall mend me—Backing horses in the sixties—I become a bookmaker—Walsall Races—Mr. Wadlow's Drone—Betting at a " Judy "

So far, I had managed this betting business with great secrecy. My chapel-going friends, my business connections—including my banker—and even my own family, excepting my brother Sam, who was thick in it with me, were kept in ignorance. But this earthquake of a calamity shook my business to its foundations, damaged my character, and exposed its hollowness to all my little wondering world.

It left me, however, reckless and defiant. I would not admit defeat ; that which had broken me should mend me again. So I continued betting, and not being able to go racing myself, others went for me, and the inevitable came. I lost my business, my friends, my beautiful home, and well-nigh broke the heart of one of the gentlest human beings that God ever lent to this earth ; and He lent her for so short a time, she did not live to see the prosperous days which were yet in store for me.

How was it possible for any ordinary backer of horses to do other than get broken in the days I am writing of ? The way for non-professional backers in these times is, may be, thorny enough, and fraught with dangers they know nothing of. But competition, I am told, has troubled even the bookmaker's profession; as in all others, it is overcrowded; hence they are compelled to lay something like fair prices, that is to say, a backer can now get what looks like fifteen shillings for his pound. It would make modern bookmakers ill and green with envy to tell of the prices we poor punters of the early sixties were compelled to take.

If, in addition to being compelled to accept ruinous prices, you happen to be cursed with a credulous disposition and an ever-open ear for " tips," depend upon it your chance of getting rich, as a punter, is very remote indeed. This was my case in those days, and occasionally I come across painful reminders of it.

Truly, in those days a man needed little beyond the proverbial " pencil and a book " to be a bookmaker, and if nature had only added to this capital a lusty voice, with a fair share of " *face*," a speedy competence was assured. A neglected education, nay, a total absence of it, was no bar. Two of the three elementary " R's " could certainly be dispensed with; so they could manage to scrawl a name and a few figures, or pay a clerk who could do it—a knowledge of figures being quite unnecessary. The bookie laid such prices, it was next to impossible for him to go wrong—six to four, each of two horses, and two to one another, with very gradually lengthening prices half-a-dozen more in the same field, was a common occurrence, and, as customers were plentiful, there was no need to keep a sharp look-out as to the state of the book, as the bookies, I believe, are obliged to do in these times.

A member of the one time well-known firm of Keeling & Gibson, hailing from Sheffield, who betted mostly to ready money, or settled on the following morning, once told me they never troubled to look at their book except to see what they had to pay when they returned home at the end of the week ; they simply turned out their pockets and divided the spoil ; and there were plenty of firms in their class who did the same.

It was, indeed, then an easy matter to make money fielding if one only played the game fair and square. How else can one understand so many bookies of the sixties piling up immense fortunes ? Rough and unpolished in manners, without education, and of poor mental calibre, they lived up to incomes far beyond that of a Lord High Chancellor, or Prime Minister of England, and dying fat and opulent, their offspring may have become the founders of country families. Who knows ?

I must now return to my own checkered life on the turf. Now in a pecuniary sense, as well as morally, I was an utter " *broker* " ; and it was in 1865, I believe, that I began to doubt whether I was not making a mistake in backing horses, and to feel that by this means I should never achieve any great success, or even get back to a tolerable means of living. I still proclaimed, however, that as the turf had broken me, the turf should mend me ; so, with my brother and W. Collins it was determined to try book-making. My friend Collins and his brother Ned had essayed it in a small way a short time before and with hopeful prospects. So now, behold, I and my brother decided to give it a trial in earnest. Our *début* was to be at Walsall, as being near home, cheaply to get at, where, possibly, we might get the patronage of a few people who would know us.

One little difficulty stood in the way—that was the tools to work with. We had pencils and a book, but no money, and even in those days, if you determined to go straight, some little capital was necessary. However, with the kindly aid of an avuncular relative, we surmounted the difficulty, and went to the famous saddlery town equipped with a big satchel and a little bank.

I was in Walsall not so long ago, and made diligent search to discover the site of the old race-course, but with little success. I knew the ancient erection called the Grand Stand was quite close to the railway station, so it must have been near what is, in these days, about the middle of that prosperous town.

It was long prior to the creation of " Tattersall's Enclosures "; still, there was an enclosure round the Grand Stand wherein most of the betting took place, but the state of our exchequer forbade any aspirations we may have had to figure there. We had to be content with the hire of a little " Judy " and a stool, on which my brother stood while holding forth and offering the odds to the assembled multitude of pitmen and artisans from the town and neighbourhood, while I sat beside the " Judy " in the capacity of clerk. My brother had a nice, open face and a presence which evidently inspired confidence—ours didn't look like " a joint " which was going to " guy," so we did a great deal more business than might have been expected for young beginners.

In the first race there were six runners, and three of them were backed at about the same price, ranging from a little under to a little over 2 to 1 ; the other three we laid outside prices varying from 5 up to 7 to 1. One of the favourites won, I think it was Volhynia ; but if my readers with any knowledge of figures will take the trouble to consider the odds, they will see we couldn't have taken much harm.

Old " Speedy " Payne won the next race on Edinburgh, and he was a 7 to 4 on chance, so we lost a trifle on that, but we ought not to have done so, because there were at least a couple of others backed at 3 to 1 each.

This brought us to the principal race of the day, and one which marks an epoch in my life. When the numbers went up we found there were five runners, and from what I afterwards came to know about it, I believe it was a nicely " cut and dried " affair.

Poor old Tom Cooper, of Birmingham, who died many years ago, was then one of the leading betting men in the Midlands, and he never was so happy as when arranging " a job " or laying against " a safe 'un," and he it was who had done the squaring in the present case, for, as he himself told me, years after, he had arranged either with the jockeys or owners the order of running in this particular race ; and what is more, it would have come off exactly as arranged, but for one little mishap.

The only horses for the race, and whose numbers went up, were The Wave, Gamecock, Charming Woman, Volhynia, and Longboat. The Wave was a very hot favourite, even money being taken freely, but as the Wave's form was by no means the best, there was plenty of money for Gamecock at 3 to 1, while the other three were well supported at 4 to 1 each.

This state of things, of course, made us feel quite comfortable ; the squaring that had taken place was nothing to us, so long as we were betting against all the horses and at a fine profit too.

But what is this we behold ?   A horse-box is on the line quite close to the course, and a horse is being hurriedly unloaded, and in a minute or so up goes another number, Mr. Wadlow's " The Drone." I don't suppose this sort of thing would be allowed now ; but strange things happened in those days, and this is an actual fact.

Now, everybody knows Mr. Wadlow was not the sort of man to be squared, and no one would know that better than old Bill Cosby, who owned The Wave, or his friend Cooper, who had done the squaring ; beside which, they didn't believe any squaring would be requisite in the case of The Drone, he was such a very execrable performer. Indeed, I am told Mr. Wadlow would have withdrawn him for a very small consideration, and offered to sell him to Cooper & Co. outright for twenty-five pounds, which they refused to give.   It was not surprising therefore that The Drone had not a single backer; the great surprise was supplied when they came to run the race, for the despised Drone won in a trot by three or four lengths, The Wave second, of course.

After this there was a most sensational race, although only a couple went to the post. There are racing men still living who will remember it, and the stir which it created in the racing world at that time. It resulted in disastrous consequences for some of those actively concerned, all of whom have, I believe, gone over to the big majority long ago.

Gamecock and Edinburgh were the runners. The former was a very popular horse in the Midlands, and there most of his triumphs were achieved. But on this occasion it was evident some one had laying orders, and so clumsily was the business done that, at the start, as much as 4 to 1 was laid on his opponent, which rather exposed the game, as such odds, if all was square, would have been simply absurd. So poor Gamecock smelt worse than " dead meat " of this description usually does.

Nevertheless, the knowing ones, who only thought they knew, who had been helping themselves accordingly, had a bit of a scare when they saw the two jockeys, Ward and Payne, putting in all they knew, and each doing the best he could to win. The scare became a veritable fright when, after racing neck and neck to the last stride, it was found that Gamecock had just beaten the favourite. The knowing ones, who had taken liberties without being really in the know, used some strong language.

It turned out, however, that this terrific finish between the two jockeys, which induced a lot of betting while it was in progress, to the discomfiture of those not in the know, was all a part of the play; for when they came to weigh in, it was found that Gamecock had carried wrong weight, and, of course, an objection was immediately laid, which was another part of the play. The takers of the odds were up in arms, and there was no end of a rumpus; and as the people concerned didn't bear the best of characters, the stewards at once suspended the jockeys and reported the case to the Jockey Club, who after an exhaustive inquiry, let Payne and Ward off with a reprimand for refusing, when called on, to give evidence, considering that the weights had been fraudulently tampered with by Kendal, the trainer, and Bilham, the owner of Gamecock. On the latter they passed the severest punishment in their power, warning him off for ever; but as Kendal was at the time under a life sentence for the Brilliant case at Chester, they could do no more with him.

Now I may say that all this did not affect us; we were betting outside the ring "all in" and "first past the post," so it was rather a good thing for us.

I shall never forget our elated condition as we went home that night. We had won something like fifty pounds, and we were fully impressed with the idea that we had discovered the El Dorado, and would want money no more in this life. Alas! there are thorns among the sweetest roses, and the fairest prospects are often beclouded, and we, like many greater people, were very quickly to find our wealth a burden. The fact is, it consisted almost entirely of silver, and when we left the train at Perry Bar we had a two-mile trudge before we reached home, and we almost quarrelled about who should carry the satchel.

After betting together for some time outside the ring, and, of course, for ready money, my brother began to tire of it, and the brothers Collins having separated, he joined Mr. W. Collins, and in the course of time theirs became one of the most respected and prominent firms in the ring.

As for me, the way was not yet made smooth enough for entrance within that magic circle, and there were many rough-and-tumble days awaiting me outside before it was so. I marred my chances through trying to find winners, instead of steadily laying against everything. The fact is, I studied " the book," and too often, when it declared that a certain horse *must* win, I could not help going a bit for that horse ; and, almost as frequently, an occult force to which I, and the like of me, were strangers, was stronger than " the book." I had yet to learn that a horse's " book " form, and even his present capabilities, are as nothing when opposed to these forces. Let me confess that I never was, at heart, a genuine book-maker. The old bad habit of backing horses clung to me, more or less, through all my turf career. This will account for my progress as a bookmaker in these early days being slow, as it will account for many other things, which, in the proper place, I shall have to unbosom myself of.

G

CHAPTER VII

An unfortunate partnership—My partner's wife—Our village
parson—Our village pubs

IT was now necessary for me to take a new partner,
and the fates chose one for me with a strange mixture
of good and bad qualities; and as the story of his life
" points a moral " which may be useful, I propose telling
it rather fully.

Fred Jackson was my daily pal, and I had grown to be
as fond of him as a brother. There was nothing about
Fred very remarkable; nothing in his looks, certainly, to
demand one's admiration. He was a little fellow with
a slight cast in one eye, and a nervous, uneasy way with
him which made one at times fidgety, and there was no
genius or force of character compelling respect, and yet
I liked him beyond and above all my friends and acquaintances of those days.

He was a merry little chap, with a good heart, a
generous disposition, and one of the sweetest tempers
that ever dwelt in a man; and I suppose that's why I
was fond of him. These good qualities are desirable
possessions for a young fellow; but unless he possesses
with them a little judgment, some strength of character

and will, he were almost better without them, for these amiable attributes in men, when not supported by those of sterner stuff, are apt to lead them astray ; to degenerate indeed, into very vices ; for is it not true that all our vices are virtues upside down, our worst faults but the negative side of good qualities ?

Fred came of a good old stock of English yeomen, who had farmed their own land from time immemorial, and nobody could tell how many John Jacksons there had been farming the broad acres of Pentlands in an unbroken succession. He was the youngest of six sons, and when his father died, the oldest of the brothers added another to the long list of John Jacksons who had held Pentlands, with its fine old red brick house, in the Queen Anne style, and its three hundred acres of unencumbered freehold land.

While this was the handsome portion of the eldest son, the others had to be content with very small fortunes, amounting to about £1,500 each.

About a year after his father's death my pal married the daughter of his father's old friend and neighbour, Moses Fitter, and the event was celebrated amid much rejoicing by the two families, for it was looked upon as a very proper and desirable match, and to merely outside observers it appeared a Heaven-made one, for the young people had been born neighbours within a month of each other, had been playmates and sort of lovers from childhood, and had many things in common. Kitty Fitter, or, as we must now call her, Mrs. Jackson, was at first sight an attractive young lady; she had an almost perfect set of features, which, when illuminated by a well-practised smile, captivated all new acquaintances and sent them away under the impression that they were fortunate in the acquisition of a charming friend. On a more intimate knowledge of the fair Kitty, however, one soon discovered that the sweet smile was not genuine, but a vapid, meaningless thing; that no soul spoke to you through the beautiful eyes, and indeed that her loveliness was the loveliness of a picture :—

"Insipid as the queen upon a card."

And a still closer acquaintance showed not only these defects but disclosed also the presence of many of the worst characteristics of human nature.

She had a vanity which exacted homage of men and made her bitterly jealous of her own sex. She could not endure any other good-looking woman near her. She was an incarnation of selfishness and therefore cruel. She was capable of the little spites and tantalising manners which are only possible to women or, I should say, to a woman of this character. While she was incapable of feeling or of understanding the true meaning of love she was a good hater, especially of those of her own sex who stood in her way, and after that, of such of the other sex as, seeing through her, refused to be captivated by her hollow coquetries.

Fred Jackson saw none of these failings in his wife; with the blindness of love he saw only the attractive outside, and he was proud of the homage and flattery she received from most of their male acquaintances. These considerations, perhaps, influenced him somewhat when he began to look about him for the best means of investing his small fortune. They had been living some months on their principal, and he felt that it was about time he got into a business of some sort ; but, like the devoted husband he was, he was anxious to consult the wishes of his pretty wife.

" I have been to Broomwater again to-day, my dear," he said, " trying to find something that would suit us, but I can find nothing that looks such a certain living as the 'Swan' Inn, here, in our own village. The lease expires in a month or so ; it's your dad's property, and he says we can have it. There is a nice little business to it, and fifty acres of good land, which I could look after."

" And you would like to bury me alive in a place like that, would you ? " asked the lady. " I'll take care that you don't. I should like the public business if you could get a proper sort of place, but not where I should scarcely ever see the face of *gentlemen*, but instead would have to draw quarts of fourpenny and cut hunks of bread and cheese all day for clodhoppers. That's not good enough for me, I can tell you. I want a proper hotel, either at Broomwater or in London."

" But consider, my dear," meekly pleaded her husband, " we have not half enough money for the sort of place you require."

" Well, then, we must get dad to help us," replied she.
" One thing is certain, I will never live at the ' Swan.' "

" Of course you won't if you have made up your mind
not to do so," replied Fred, with more bitterness in his
tone than the young wife was accustomed to hear in
these early days of matrimony. " It does not matter
about me, of course. What I like or dislike is not of the
slightest consequence."

The young wife looked at her husband for the space of a
minute with a strangely puzzled expression, as though
she rather doubted her sense of hearing. Surely this
could not be the meek and subservient young man she had
already come to look upon as her abject slave ; and when
she fully realised the matter, she burst into a fit of tears.

" You are a cruel wretch, Fred," she sobbed, " and
I'll go back to my father, and tell him what a brute you
are ; that's what I'll do ! "

" Don't be foolish, Kitty, my dear," said he, wondering
what dreadfully cruel deed he had perpetrated to bring
all this trouble about his ears. " You know I don't
wish you to live anywhere or do anything you don't like.
I'll go to Broomwater again to-morrow and try to find
something you would like. I'll do anything you wish."

This complete capitulation seemed to satisfy, for the
moment, Mrs. Jackson, so they kissed and became friends
again, and it was arranged that she should accompany
her husband the following day to the great town of
Broomwater in quest of a business of some sort, which
should be not only profitable but consonant with the

wishes and fancies of pretty Kitty. In due course this journey was taken, and, after much parleying on the part of agents and solicitors, the result was that Fred and his sprightly wife became the host and hostess of the "Nile" Hotel in the pretty little village of Mossleigh, which was the home of several families of sporting men, and was also, considering its size and proximity to its great neighbour Broomwater, an exceedingly lively little village. And in those days it was a real village. The small ancient church, with its ivy-covered walls, its low Norman tower, also clad in ivy, and from age and associations alike sacred, was large enough to seat the whole population of the village proper, as well as the squire, his family, and the numerous servants at the neighbouring hall. The parson belonged to a species then fast becoming extinct, and now utterly so. He was a rosy-faced, jolly old fellow, whose most marked characteristic was an intense love of a good horse, and few men knew one—when he saw it—better than our parson ; and I have never met with a man with such a profound knowledge of the thorough-bred and all the various strains of blood as Parson Davids.

None of your strait-laced sort was our parson ; he entered into all the sports and pastimes of his people. Some of the more unfriendly of his parishioners declared that these matters occupied too much of his attention, to the exclusion of more serious functions. He didn't think himself too good to step into the sanded parlour of the "Old Bull"—next door to the church—which was an institution only second in importance to the church itself, and there discuss parish matters or less serious affairs, over a glass of grog. And it was not an uncommon thing, strange as it may seem in these awfully pious times, to find him making up a rubber at whist, or, what he loved better still, playing five-card cribbage with old Tom Dickson, the clerk, sexton, bell-ringer, and village carpenter. His people generally liked him all the better for these free-and-easy habits, but the few spiteful villagers before alluded to were terribly scandalised, and I suppose it was one of those who spread the report that the parson, who had dropped into a gentle doze while presiding over a parish meeting, on being rudely awakened, cried out :

" Fifteen two, fifteen four, a pair's six, and one for his nob ! "

The " Nile " was situated some distance from the church, and in appearance and habits was totally unlike the " Old Bull " Inn. It was a great, big, square, modern building, with four stories, having a lofty smoke-room, bar-parlour, and billiard saloon, and it disdained the humble inn, and got itself known as the " Nile " Hotel. It had been built to accommodate a new village, which was no village at all, but a jerry-built, stuccoed suburb of the neighbouring big town, which was fast arising in its vicinity. A good many of the new-comers, like their new houses, had fine outside appearances, stucco fronts, imitation facings, instead of good, honest brick and stone ; and their inside walls all lath and plaster, unsubstantial and unsound.

The new gentry were too respectable to keep the company of the parson and the old-fashioned " Knopes," as the villagers were called, whom nothing could allure from the " Old Bull," its little rooms with sanded floors, painted walls and white-washed ceilings, low-roofed and cosy. So such of them as were not afraid of going to any public-house patronised the new hotel, with its fine billiard saloon, its pleasure grounds, gardens, lawns, and rustic arbours, and many a happy afternoon have I spent among these people on the beautiful bowling-green, which, alas ! has long since been given up to the ruthless hand of the jerry-builder. And it was here also that I first met the hero of my story and his weak but pretty wife.

For about a year things went on fairly well at the "Nile." The charming young landlady had turned the heads of all the youthful swells in the neighbourhood, and some of their elders, who ought to have known better, spent far too much of their time, under her fascinating influence, in the bar-parlour ; this especially being so while Fred was away from home, attending the numerous race-meetings in the locality ; for I must sorrowfully confess he would journey with me and my friends to all the races within a reasonable distance of his home. He began to back horses too freely, and I frequently warned him that it was a practice beset with considerable danger for clever men, possessing advantages which he lacked ; and I more than hinted that he was not likely to shine in that business— was, indeed, much more likely to come to no boots, and perhaps a bad ending. But inordinate conceit character- ises all young beginners at the game ; how else can you account for the incredulous and almost pitying smile with which they invariably receive one's warnings? It is clear they believe themselves capable of standing where all others fall, and of doing that which ninety-nine out of every hundred of their fellows fail to do.

When Fred had a good day he was loud in proclaiming it; he told everybody how many winners he had found, and largely discounted his winnings by lavishly treating all comers. When he lost he said little about it, he was quiet and subdued enough; he treated himself then, and drank to keep up his spirits. And so, I fear, he contracted a couple of foolish habits at the same time, either being, singly, likely enough to bring a man to grief, and when combined certain to do so.

Mrs. Jackson did not discourage her husband in his race-going; on the contrary she rather liked it. She may not have been morally a very bad woman, perhaps not so bad as some of the seemingly modest prudes who made free with her name, and so severely commented upon her conduct in her husband's absence; but she was a married flirt—a most dangerous creature, to be avoided, ay, and even hated, by men who care for their own peace.

" What are you looking so glum about? " I remarked to Jackson, as we walked down the lanes from Lichfield race-course to the city.

" Well, to tell you the truth, I've been making a fool of myself? " he replied.

" And is that anything new? " I couldn't help observing, for I had seen enough of what he had been doing in the ring to convince me that he had lost a good deal more than he could afford. " You needn't tell me ; I can see you have had a bad day, and you expect me to sympathise with you. Have not I told you, over and over again, that you are not made of the stuff successful backers are made of ? You don't know a race-horse from a donkey, nor a sharp from a juggins ; you think you're a sharp, and you are the veriest jay ; and I'm telling you once more, if you don't pitch up backing horses, you'll be on your uppers in a few years."

" And yet I can see fellows about who are getting tons of money at the game," he answered, " and some of them, a few years ago, were jockeys' valets, card-sellers, and touts, if not worse."

" That is so," I replied, " but you aren't made that way, and, you can take my word for it, you will never do as they have done. Don't I tell you that I know lots of swells with opportunities you can never have—not jays, mind you, but clever fellows in their way, having trainers, and jockeys, and horses of their own, and plenty of capital to work the show, and yet nine out of every ten of them go broke at it. Pitch it, Fred, my lad, pitch it before you join the band of brokers."

" I'm afraid I've qualified for membership already," he replied dejectedly. " In fact, that's what I wanted to talk about when I asked you to walk down with me ; but I'm really ashamed to tell you what a fool I've been, after all the good advice you have given me. I haven't only lost more than I—I—oh, hang it, I can't tell you ! "

" Oh, out with it ! " I said, beginning to feel somewhat

alarmed, the little man looked so distressed. " You haven't lost more than you will be able to pay, I hope ? "

" No, that isn't it exactly. I shall be able to pay all my debts of honour, but I'm afraid the spirit merchant and one or two others must wait ; but it's worse than that. I was fool enough to accept a bill three months ago to help poor old Scooper out of a mess ; in fact, it was to prevent him being broken up. He told me I should never be troubled about it, for, long before it came due, he should be receiving a lot of money, and then he would take the bill out of the money-lender's hands. A week ago I got a writ from the money-lender for this bill, and unless it's paid in two or three days, my wife will get to know about it, and there'll be the very devil to pay."

" You idiot ! " I couldn't help saying, " to go and put your name to a bill for a lazy shicer like old Ned. Well, you are a fool ! How much is it ? "

" The bill was a hundred pounds, but the interest and expenses will make it another twenty, I suppose," answered he.

" And what have you lost here to-day ? " I asked.

" About forty pounds."

" And what right had you to come here and lose forty pounds ? " I asked, quite savagely, for I felt very much annoyed, having helped him out of a similar scrape on a smaller scale, six months before, when he solemnly promised he would do nothing of the kind again if I would only help him to keep this matter from the know-ledge of his wife, of whom he was in mortal fear, and so soon to rush into the same folly was sorely trying to my scanty stock of patience.

"Well, the fact is," he said, "I thought I might have a bit of luck, and run into enough to settle with this infernal money-lender; but that's how it always is, one never does get any luck when it's so badly wanted. The only folks who get luck are those with plenty of stuff."

"Oh, luck be blowed!" I replied. "Don't twaddle to me about luck; you go and act like a blithering idiot, and when the natural consequences come, you begin to whine about your bad luck. Oh, go to the devil," and, in my passion and impatience, I went striding on in front of him, and only when I had nearly reached the verge of the city did I turn my head to look for him. He was nowhere to be seen. I was alarmed, for I was sure he was attached to me, and I knew he would take to heart any harshness on my part, for in spite of weakness and vacillation and other bad qualities, he was tender-hearted and sensitive to a degree.

As I have said, I felt alarmed; but I didn't know what to do for the best. I felt I could not go on without him, so I chartered a cab which was returning empty to the course, and went back the way we had come, looking in every direction for him. When we reached the common I caught sight of him walking across it, right away from the course and the people, and in the direction of a wood I could see in the distance. I very quickly came up with him.

"Where do you think you are going?" I asked.

" Where you directed me, I suppose," was the sullen reply, while he never took his eyes off the ground.

" Don't be a fool. Get into the cab."

After a little while I succeeded in getting him to do so, and very soon we were at the " Swan," in front of a good dinner and a bottle of Moët's, under the influence of which he became quite cheerful again. I induced my brother to help, and at eleven o'clock that night, when I parted with him at the door of his own house, he shook my hand very warmly.

" You and your brother have made a new man of me," he said. " I'll stick to business, and back no more horses, at any rate till you are paid—and I shall always be grateful for what you have done for me to-night."

CHAPTER VIII

Old-time betting "Judies"—A hot corner at Liverpool—How I
   was rescued—I dissolve the partnership—My partner's sad
   end

POOR old Fred! I am sure he intended to do all he
promised, and the tear that he couldn't help my detecting
in that queer cross eye of his was the result of as genuine
emotion as ever moved a human heart; and yet, so weak
was his nature, very soon all his good resolves were thrown
to the winds, and he was backing horses as freely as ever.
I had another turn with him, and then he confided to
me a secret which I already suspected; he was not happy
at home. Would I help him to become a bookmaker
in ever such a small way, so he might travel to all the
meetings, leaving his wife to attend to the hotel, which
she had told him she could manage better without him?

In vain I tried to dissuade him from this course;
he had made up his mind, and he would give it a trial.
It happened that just at the time I was betting outside
the ring at what was known as a " judy "; that is, a
betting establishment on the course very like a Punch
and Judy show. These erections are not allowed in these
days, as they were construed into places for the purpose
of betting many years ago, and abolished; but at the time

95

I am writing of they were common enough ; some of the bookies carrying their own shows about with them, while others rented them from men who travelled to all the meetings with a large stock of " judies." These men would pay, at certain important places, large sums to the clerks of the courses for rent of the land on which they erected these small betting boxes. This system gave place to more substantial and commodious offices, which were erected alongside the betting rings, one side fronting to the ring and the other to the outside public ; a man standing on a stool inside the ring doing business with one set of clients, his pal taking on the outsiders in the same way, while a clerk, or sometimes two, sat inside the judy. Some very respectable and substantial men bet to ready money in this way, and made considerable fortunes at it. I could point to some who, at the present moment, are among the best advertised people on the turf, men of wealth and great respectability, whom I can well remember betting outside these judies, or exercising the humbler office inside. Let me cite as an illustration the one name which most readily occurs to me, that of Robert Topping—the most eminent S.P. man in the world. I remember one year when Steel and Peach, the greatest of all bookmakers at that time, rented the whole of the land at Doncaster or York which was available for this purpose, and set up a great number of these betting boxes, and let them to bookmakers of good standing for whom they risked little in guaranteeing them, charging £50 and upwards for the use of each box, and some of the best known names in the ring—their own among them—were painted above these boxes. Well, it was not at one of these important places that I and my friend, Fred Jackson, proposed to start in partnership as bookies, but at the earlier and humbler sort. Our united capital was not large, but he undertook to raise and be ready with fifty pounds as his contribution to it.

So the capital and stock-in-hand of this new firm was provided; this consisted of four upright pieces of wood, spiked at the bottom to drive into the ground, brass rods to hold them in their places, five or six yards of green baize to wrap round it, a flaming banner of scarlet cloth, on which was inscribed in large characters this device:

" Dyke and Jackson :
All In, Run or Not."

A huge black satchel, with the same device on its face in gilt letters ; and with this an orange-coloured leather strap, a couple of inches wide, which was to be suspended round my neck, and carry the satchel. Then there was a large square book, on the cover of which the name of the firm also appeared ; and an immense green gig umbrella formed a roof to the establishment.

For the first week or two business was not very brisk, as we were unknown to the public ; still, we managed to win a few pounds over the expenses each week, which were equally divided, and Fred, after the manner of his kind, began to indulge in rosy dreams. It was Liverpool Autumn Meeting, and the new firm, full of the hopes

H

which come from success, even so limited as ours had been, bet through the first day with harmless results, and I had not been obliged to ask Jackson for any money.

On the second day things went badly on the three first races. The favourite won each of them, and we lost about forty pounds, which I paid out of my own stock; but before we began to bet on the next race, I gave Jackson notice that if we lost again he must begin to pull out some money.

In the fourth race there were ten runners, and among them an unnamed colt, Buntline out of Lassie. In so large a field I thought I might safely lay six to four anything; so, being anxious to get on with the business, I cried out, " I'll lay fifteen pounds to ten on the field! " Immediately a crafty punter standing by, and who made a living out of young beginners, rushed a ten-pound note into my hand, saying, " I'll have that Buntline Colt," and before the bet was booked I found I had been too hasty, for the general offer was even money Buntline. I then laid a number of smaller bets against the same horse at evens to equalise the bad bet, and thinking that, of course, they would be certain to back others among so many runners.

" Here, what price Lassie colt ? " asked a square-headed gentleman who stood by with a fiver in his hand.

" Ten pounds to five," I replied, thinking I wouldn't again commit the blunder of opening my mouth too wide to begin with, which blunder had somewhat worried and confused me, and I was rather surprised to see how eagerly the offer was closed with, and also how quickly some of the bystanders followed suit, and it was not until I had laid more than twenty pounds against Lassie that it occurred to me that it was the same as Buntline; and when we realised that we had laid against this horse something more than fifty pounds, and had only got two or three sovereigns out of the other nine to pay it with, we were in a dreadful state, especially poor me. I broke out into a cold perspiration, trembling in every limb, and became, in rapid succession, all sorts of colours. I could no longer stand firmly on the high stool; the big satchel, although nearly empty, seemed dragging me down to the earth, so I sat on it, a picture of misery, awaiting events.

"You will be ready with fifty pounds, Fred!" I gasped in whispers; "I feel sure the favourite will win." And the looks of two or three of my clients, who had never lost sight of me, or moved far from me since their bets were made, was by no means reassuring. Fred, however, did not seem to feel our position half so keenly, for his naturally sanguine disposition came to his relief.

"Don't funk," he said; "I don't think he's sure to win; we've nine chances to his one, and we——" but before he could finish his sentence there was a cry, "They're off!" and I jumped again on my stool excitedly to watch the race.

At the distance it was seen there were only two in it, and they came away by themselves, locked together, neck and neck. They struggled thus towards the winning-post; now Buntline seeming to get his head in front;

and the next stride the outsider, struggling gamely and helped by the almost superhuman efforts of his jockey, had the best of it ; and so they passed the post, everybody crying, " Dead heat ! dead heat ! "

Looking eagerly towards the number board, where, unfortunately for our young firm and all our rosy dreams, Buntline's number was hoisted as the winner, I sat down again on my stool, feeling at that moment that a brandy-and-soda would be cheap at half-a-crown.

" Fred, you must give me fifty ; we are dead broke."

No reply came from Fred. I stood up and looked inside the judy. It was empty. Fred had gone. The crowd began to gather around me, awaiting the welcome cry, " All right ! " before they could draw their winnings.

When I found that Fred had deserted his post, I didn't know what to make of it. I could not for a moment believe that my pal had deserted me and left me to the mercy of an enraged mob ; but what could it mean ? He had gone, that much was certain ; and with him had gone the large square book in which the bets were entered, so that if any good neighbour would lend me the money, or even if I had it in my pocket, it would be impossible for me to settle with the rough customers already gathered round me, and who, in another two or three minutes, would be clamorously demanding their winnings. There were yet these few minutes of grace left ; so I mounted my stool again, looking wildly in every direction for a glimpse of Jackson, with the means of escape from this dangerous situation. There was no sign of him anywhere, and escape for myself, even had I been so disposed, was out of the question—was, indeed, utterly impossible—for I was now surrounded by the enemy. " All right ! " being bellowed out by the man employed by the bookies for this purpose, they began at once to discharge their liabilities as their tickets were handed up.

My knees knocked against each other, and every fibre of me trembled with fear as I heard the ominous cry. I knew too well what it meant if I failed to satisfy the demands of this pack of hungry wolves crowding about me.

" Fifteen pounds," said the sharp who had done me with the unfair 2 to 1 bet, and who was the first to demand payment.

" I must ask you to wait a few minutes till my pal comes back ; he's got the book," said I, scarcely knowing what I said ; and still standing on my stool looking wildly about me for my partner.

There was a good deal of murmuring, but for the present no hostile movement on the part of the punters. Five minutes passed, the other bookies had finished paying out, and had become interested in the proceedings in front of our shop ; and seeing there was something wrong, there gathered around quite a crowd of punters and loafers, who had no interest in the matter apart from the desire to see a row, or to help, maybe, in the baiting of a poor wretch standing on the stool, white and trembling, and almost palsied with fear.

As the minutes went the murmurs of the crowd became angry growls, and violence would have been resorted to but for the interference of the owner of the next judy, who told the mob that he believed the young men were respectable, and meant paying. This answered for a few minutes longer; but it was painfully clear to me that the patience of my clients was nearly exhausted, and they were edging closer upon me. I saw fierce eyes intent upon the satchel which hung from the broad strap around my neck; I knew there would be a struggle first for that, and then for me.

Meantime, while this scene was being acted before the betting office of the new firm, Fred was on the course at the side of the principal betting enclosure, whither he had flown the instant he saw the favourite had won, and where he was making frantic efforts to get a glimpse of my brother in the ring. When the race was over my brother had gone to the telegraph office, in those days some distance away, so was not to be found. When he returned to the ring he was told of Fred wanting him on the course; he ran down to him, and found him in a pitable condition.

" For God's sake," said he, " come with me down to the ' joint ' at once! We haven't enough to pay, and I'm afraid they'll kill poor Dyke, if they haven't already done it. I'll explain all afterwards."

There was no time for question or explanation; Sam ran out of the ring and made for me as fast as his legs would carry him, Fred running by his side, deadly pale with fear and excitement. Fifty yards from the judy he could see there was a row; when he reached the crowd he saw me in the midst of it, my coat nearly torn off, no hat upon my head, and other signs of ill-usage; about me a couple of policemen, who, mercifully for me, happened for once to be where they were wanted, had hold of me, and were valiantly protecting me as well as they could from the violence of the crowd.

My brother pushed his way into the midst of them.

"What the devil are you doing, you cowardly ruffians?" he shouted. I could see he was known by some of the mob. "Couldn't you give them a few minutes' grace while his pal came to get some more money?"

Some of them, when they saw the turn things were taking, seemed a bit ashamed, and slunk into the background.

I was glad to find my brother was in time to prevent my being seriously hurt, although I had been roughly handled.

"And now, Jackson," my brother said, "you get into the box and let's have everybody paid; and let me tell you, gentlemen," he said, turning to the crowd, "you needn't be afraid of betting with these men—they won't bet what they can't pay."

In two or three minutes all the claims were satisfied, and the numbers were hoisted for the next race.

"Now, then, my lads, bet away and don't be afraid," he said, "I'll be with you the minute the race is over."

With this he ran back to his own business. It was evident the row and his opportune appearance and promises had been an advertisement for us, for on his return after the race he found we had been doing a very much larger business than before, and it was also a profitable one. We had laid the winner several times, but had won about twenty-five pounds on the race.

" Dash it at them, Dyke," he said, " give your winnings a chance ; this row will do you no harm at the finish. I can see."

" But I want to tell you something before I go any farther," replied I.

He had no time to listen to my explanation then, so he asked me to leave it till we could come to his lodgings in the evening.

After he had dined that evening, the new firm went to my brother looking so uncommonly serious that he thought we must have had the bad luck to lay the outsider which had given all such a " skinner " on the last race of the day. His first question was :

" You surely didn't lay the last winner ? "

" No, we didn't," I answered, very gravely.

" Well, what did you win ? "

" Oh, all we took—about forty-five pounds," was the answer ; and without another word I took out a parcel and placed it in his hands. " You'll find there," I said, in the same serious tones, " all I had from you. I shall never be able to tell you how grateful I am to you for bringing me help at that moment, for I believe you saved my life. But I've done."

" What does all this mean ? " my brother asked, turning to Jackson, who all through the business had never uttered a word.

" I am to blame, I know," he answered ; " but I was obliged to use, in the business at home, the money I had received from Dyke, and I thought perhaps we mightn't want any ; and if we did——"

" If you did you could come to me for it," Sam interrupted fiercely, and I am afraid he said several things in his passion which would not look well set down here. It was clear to my brother he had acted most dishonourably, and that I was quite justified in throwing him up, and no amount of snivelling and vehement promising on the part of Fred could shake my resolution.

I have often thought how different might have been the after life and the end of Jackson if he had only had the courage to keep in his new business what belonged to it, or even to confess that his wife had got it from him. And once again his curse was weakness. He had persuaded himself the money wouldn't be wanted ; he never for a moment intended working such mischief for himself or his friend.

I was this time so thoroughly annoyed with the conduct of Jackson that I didn't see him or go into the " Nile " for several months, but I heard some very bad accounts of him. He had got into fresh difficulties of a pecuniary kind, and was constantly quarrelling with his wife and her relatives ; and, perhaps driven thitherwards by these things, he was now drinking worse than ever. Old Moses Fitter, his father-in-law, had advanced a good deal of money when they bought the " Nile," and, since, was threatening to put in force the powers he held over him, and this at last the old man did, and Jackson had to fly from his angry creditors, for, of course, he was too weak to meet them, and so I lost sight of him as did also his wife and all his family.

All the remainder of that season went, and the following winter, and there was no news of him. His friends concluded either he was dead or had gone abroad. When he left there was a pretty little one-year-old daughter, whom he loved with an intensity one could scarcely expect to find in a nature so weak.

And Mrs. Jackson was sure if he were alive he would come back for love of that child, if not for its mother's sake.

Now and again I had fancied I saw him flitting about among the crowds on a race-course, and once, when I was being whirled out of a railway station, I thought I got just a glimpse of him through the window of the cab. I pulled up instantly, jumped out, and sought among the throng for him; but if it was he, he had disappeared.

The spring, with its precious promises and all its beautiful budding life, had passed, and the fair face of the earth was bathed in all the glory of summer. I was staying at the pretty village of Charlton for the Goodwood week.

It was my custom to walk with my friends from our lodgings up to the races, and on the last day of the meeting we had left soon after breakfast, and were sauntering quietly up the course. We had arrived at that part devoted to the use of the gipsies and other followers of racing—the nomads who live—

" Homeless, ragged, and tann'd,
Under the changeful sky—"

the class one meets with at all the principal races, even
when widely apart and about whom the mystery has
always been what they live on, and how they get from place
to place.

The gipsies were busy pegging up the sheets for Aunt
Sallies, arranging the cocoanuts, empty bottles, and
other contrivances for turning an honest penny and
affording the rustics sport. The vagabond tribe, unwashed
and ragged, lay in every direction, where I suppose they
had lain through the night.

Passing one of the gipsies' caravans, I was struck
by the appearance of something lying under it, something
which looked at first sight like a heap of filthy rags ; yet
from the rag heap there gleamed a pair of human eyes
strangely familiar. After we had passed, I couldn't help
remarking to one of my friends : " If Mrs. Jackson hadn't
told me they had good reasons for believing her husband
dead, I should certainly think those eyes we saw, under
yon gipsy's van, belonged to poor old ' Fred.' "

My friends pooh-poohed the idea. The eyes haunted
me when I was in the ring, and as there was an hour before
racing began, I made my way back to the caravan.
When about thirty yards from it I saw a bundle of rags
pull itself up and scuttle away. I felt sure the being
which dwelt in that mass of rags had seen me making
directly for it, and had flown to avoid me. Swiftly as
possible I rushed on to the ground ; there was no sign

of him. I went round every vehicle and shed and booth without finding him, and yet I knew he could not be far away. Suddenly a happy thought struck me. He would have had just time to run up the bank, get over the fence and hide himself in the adjacent wood ; there I went on the instant, and the moment I reached the top of the bank I saw the object I was in search of, lying in a heap on the other side of the fence. In a moment I was by his side. He was exhausted by the effort he had made, and lay with his eyes closed and breathing heavily. I was afraid he was dying. I saw a decent-looking old gipsy woman, sitting on the top of the bank, nursing a tiny member of her tribe. I called to her and got her to fetch me some brandy. Before she returned he opened his eyes, and whatever doubts I may have had on the subject vanished. I knew it was Fred Jackson.

" Why, whatever has brought you to this condition ? " I asked gently ; and seeing he was struggling with some strong emotion, I added : " But don't try to talk yet. You shall have a drop of brandy and something to eat, and then you can tell me all about it."

In a few minutes the old gipsy returned, and with her a powerful but good-natured fellow, her son. After he had tasted the brandy he seemed revived a little ; then, turning his hungry eyes upon me, his pent-up feelings gave way, and bursting into a passion of tears, his first words were :

" My child, my little child, how is she ? "

I was myself almost choking with emotion, but I gave him such soothing answer as I could.

I arranged with the good gipsy to get a fly and drive him down to Chichester at once, getting him there a lodging, medical attendance, and whatever he might have instant need of; and after the races were over I hurried down to him. He had been comfortably cared for, was now clean and wholesome, and in a good bed, which was a luxury he had not enjoyed for a long time. Between fits of terrible coughing he told the part of his sad story I was unacquainted with. It appeared he had dodged me, on race-courses and at railway stations, many times; and till now had always succeeded in avoiding detection. As long as he was strong enough he had earned a scanty living by fetching and carrying for the judy-builders on the course, and doing odd jobs at the stations. How he had lived and crawled about during the last few months he couldn't tell.

I told him I should write at once to his family and let them know where he was. This he strongly opposed and begged me with tears not to do so.

" Let it be a few days at least. I couldn't bear to see her or any of them just at present." And he pleaded so earnestly, I yielded. I have always thought he knew more than the doctor who had been called in, and more than I suspected, for in four days after, when his friends did see him, he slept calmly, his face had lost its care-worn look, there were no wrinkles on his pale, cold forehead; his queer odd eyes were closed for ever.

CHAPTER IX

A famous Inn—Notable " Brums "—A case of sudden death—
the ruling passion—A short boxing bout—" Nibbler "—
Birch—Palmer the poisoner and Bob Brettle

AT length the way had been made smooth, and I had
risen above the " judy " style of betting, and was,
although as yet in a humble way, a regular member of the
ring, and betting to considerably more money. I had left
all my old associations of chapel and class-room a long
way behind me, and mingled, even when not racing, with
the sporting men, " peds " and boxers of my native town,
and, of course, spent a good part of my time at their
resorts, where I became acquainted with many men
notable in their way ; among whom were some very
eccentric, droll characters ; others clever and unscrupulous, who became, in after years, conspicuous on the
turf ; and if they reflected small honour on the good old
town of Birmingham, they afforded interesting subjects
for the student of human nature, and this shall be my
excuse for giving them a place here.

The house I mostly frequented was perhaps the most
respectable amongst these haunts of card-players and
gamblers ; it was known as the " Coach and Horses,"

in Bell Street, demolished years ago to make way for market extensions. Nearly a century earlier this was the most celebrated tavern in Birmingham. Poet Freeth, a great local celebrity, was the host, and a very clever man too. Nightly, we are told, he gathered about him a good deal of the intellect of the town, discussing not only Birmingham matters, but high affairs of State; diversifying these controversies with literary discourse, wherein, naturally, the poet's own works figured largely.

Freeth's works were well read in his day, were typical of the times, and thought much of; many of them being really very clever. I fancy, however, if you wanted to read them now you would have to do as I have done for that purpose, pay a visit to the British Museum.

In the days which concern us the old house was kept by as honourable a man as ever conducted " a pub " or any other business, although he added to this occupation the making of books on the Derby, and other big future events in racing. Unlike too many of his trade, he discouraged excessive drinking, and although his tavern was frequented by all the big gamblers of the town, he would be no party to sharp or shady practices of any kind; and woe to the man, were he the best customer he had, who attempted such. A good, all-round, honest sport was old Bill Wills, straight and true as the bore of a gunbarrel, if not as smooth; an upright, sound-headed, kind-hearted man.

Among the nightly visitors at the " Coach and Horses " was a big fat man named Kemp, in his way a character.

He possessed a great lion-like head, and a strong, intellectual face.

Coming, I believe, of a highly respectable family, Kemp started life with a good education and brilliant prospects, and with these had natural abilities which might have helped him to any goal he chose to aim at. Unfortunately for him, cards enslaved him ; he became infatuated with whist ; in fact, nothing less than a devotee, and, as was natural with a man of such mental capacity, he was great at this one game, or science, as he would have it. He was the subtle master of all its traps and intricacies, and his memory was even more wonderful than his perfect knowledge of the art. To say that, during the progress of a game, he never forgot a single card that was played, and who played it, is a small matter. I have known him, when a dispute had arisen over a particular game, perhaps a day afterwards, on being appealed to, go through that particular game, playing, card by card, all the thirteen tricks. He was pre-eminently the greatest whist player I have ever met ; but alas ! what a price he had paid for his pre-eminence !

Whist had absorbed all his faculties, ruined his business, and made him what he was at the time of which I am writing—a poor, broken-down, semi-professional card-player, sitting night after night waiting for the means to live next day. He was the fairest player in the world, and never gambled to any extent at the game, and often gentlemen of means came to play with him, and for the pleasure of being his partner guaranteed him against loss, while the half-crowns won were his own. I learnt my whist off him, and while I admit having spent many happy hours by its means, I must confess that I have, at times, regretted that I ever came under its fascinating influence, it is such a murderer of time.

Among the old Birmingham sports of the better kind who were found occasionally at the " Coach and Horses," and whom I saw a good deal of there and elsewhere, was old William Aston, the great button-maker, and one of the most eccentric men I have ever met. He was not a heavy better at anything, and I never knew him do much at horse-racing or cards, yet he was in his way an inveterate gambler. His delight was tossing the coin—heads or tails—for a sovereign, and occasionally for larger stakes and so much had this habit become a passion with him, he indulged it at all sorts of incongruous times and places.

I remember on one occasion when an eminent lawyer in Birmingham, known as a good sportsman and a shining light in legal circles, was in the middle of an eloquent speech before the Judge of the County Court. Suddenly a bit of paper was put into his hand, containing these words in Mr. A.'s well-known scrawl.

" I am waiting below for you ; come at once."

The lawyer paused in his speech, while he glanced at the paper, then turning to the judge, without the slightest hesitation, he said :

" Will your honour kindly excuse me for two minutes while I speak just one word with a person outside ? It is, I understand, a case of ' sudden death,' but I will not keep

I

the Court more than a minute or two." Then rushing into the street in wig and gown, he found Mr. A. in his brougham ready for him, and in the familiar position with a sovereign on the back of his hand.

" Head ! " cried the lawyer.

" Take it," replied A., uncovering the coin, which, it seemed, the lawyer had won. " Drive on, coachman." This was all that passed, and in one minute the lawyer had resumed his speech.

Mr. A. was not what you would call a practical joker, yet for many years he indulged in a joke which seemed to afford him immense pleasure, and among those who knew him it could do no harm ; although he really bet little or nothing on horse-racing, he would turn up occasionally at the resorts of the men who do, and start knocking the favourites out, or perhaps backing them for tremendous amounts, both sides apparently booking the bets in all seriousness, while, as it was well understood among them, it was all chaff. This old joke of his, however, on one occasion resulted in most painful consequences, which effectually prevented its repetition. One night, during the Birmingham races, while the town was full of betting men from all parts, he entered a public place, and commenced, what appeared to the strangers, a savage onslaught on the favourite for the Derby, finishing by laying some very big bets at about twice the market odds. So the strange betting men who were present, thinking it was his brother Charles, the biggest better in the town, rushed off to the telegraph office, wiring to their friends in

Manchester and elsewhere, that Aston, the great Birmingham bookmaker, was knocking out the Derby favourite, and before the error could be corrected a good deal of damage was done.

Aston was the friend and patron of the hosts of all the famous hostelries in the good old town. He subscribed liberally for the benefit of everything and everybody, and never declined to become a member of sick societies, beanfeasts, money clubs, or, indeed, any kind of club or association. At the termination of a money club where he had £50 coming to him, the worthy host, Dick Parsons, went to his house to take him the money. He was at the time very ill; in fact, it was shortly before he died. Parsons, putting the £50 in sovereigns on a table by the old man's bed, said :

" I've brought you £50, your chance in the money club, Mr. Aston ; but I'm very sorry to find you so ill."

" You'll oblige me, Dick, if you'll go ' sudden death ' double or quits the lot."

The great button-maker and his daily companion and chum, Richard Walker, one of the largest percussion cap-makers in the world, throughout many years indulged in a very curious practice. Every day, at their first meeting, instead of the usual meaningless conventionalities, one silently took a sovereign out of his pocket, placed it on the back of his hand, and the other named head or tail for its value. This was their manner of daily greeting.

There came a time when good old Dick was stricken

with a mortal sickness. Just before he died he was seized by the desire to see his old friend. When, awe-stricken and on tip-toes, he entered the chamber, the sick man was dozing, or unconscious, but Aston could not help observing that a bright sovereign shone on the little table by the side of the bed. By and by Dick opened his dulled eyes, and recognising his visitor, with some effort he reached for the sovereign, and without a word placed it on the back of his hand in the usual manner, only with those strangely dim eyes asking his friend to name it.

" Not now, not now ! I can't, Dick, I can't ! " sobbed the tender-hearted old man.

" You must, Bill, for the last time," murmured the dying man, and seeing that it would comfort him, Bill called and lost, and poor old Dick smiled faintly, having demonstrated how strong was his ruling passion, even in death.

Excepting Kemp, there was perhaps not a more frequent visitor at this old pub than my poor old friend, and some time partner in the bookmaking business, Billy Thornton. He was a great card-player in almost all its branches, and a born gambler, who would bet on anything at any time or place. A one-eyed, dry old stick was Billy, and very clever. We were playing whist late one night, or perhaps it would be safer to say it was early in the morning, for it was anterior to Mr. Bruce's Early Closing Bill. Thornton was losing money, so was in no humour to brook the sneers and interference of a big bully who was present—a bully and blackguard at best when sober, but when half drunk a terror to everybody. We were all amazed to see Billy suddenly rise from his seat, and challenge the bully to turn out of the house and fight ; for although we knew he had been able to " put them up " in his early days, and was reputed quick as lightning, we felt certain he could have no chance against his burly opponent, for he had but indifferent light in his one eye, was double the other's age, and not more than half his weight, and certainly had the appearance of a consumptive. So we did all we could to keep him in the house, but without avail, for fight he would.

The big bully was not manly enough to decline the unequal contest, but readily went out and stripped for the fray. The instant they faced each other Billy flew at the big one like a wild cat, and was all over him in an instant ; and before he knew where he was, or had thought of beginning to fight, he was pasted all over his face. It didn't last more than two minutes, and then we saw the old man putting his coat on as he walked into the house, breathless, and half dead with the terrible effort.

" Come out of that ! " shouted the bully ; " come out and finish the fight ! "

" No, I shan't fight any more," replied Billy. " I'll give you best."

My old friend's racing career, like his fighting, was of the spasmodic order—fitful, uncertain, and unbusinesslike. In the whole course of my experience I never met with a man who was so continually " a broker." He never appeared, from start to finish, to make any headway. I don't know how many times in each of all the many years I knew him, poor old Bill was " a broker."   In fact, his was a case of chronic brokerage.   For the sake of his many good qualities somebody was always ready to help him to start again.   He was a notable example of how bad luck—as he called it—will stick to a man.   I will give one illustration of the many which occurs to me.

The day before Royal Ascot commenced all his neighbours and friends who had business there made their way to their quarters, Sunning Hill, Sunning Dale, or other of the delightful villages adjacent to the course so as to be ready when the ball was set rolling on the following day. Not so Billy ; a good friend had provided him with a really nice little bank, and a clerk to book for him ; but he must needs stop in Birmingham to play cards on Monday night, and even into the early hours of Tuesday morning, hence he was late for the 7.30 train. He managed, after bad luck, or otherwise, to arrive on the course when three races had been run, and three hot favourites beaten. Was ever such provoking luck known ? Now mark the folly and superstition of this clever man. He had got too late to take advantage of betting against three beaten favourites, therefore he would not bet against any other favourites that day. After three such " turn-ups " it would be like his luck for every favourite to win if he started to lay, so he thought he would dodge fate, turn round, and back favourites for the remainder of the day. This he did, and the " turn-ups " continued. Not one single favourite won on the day ; so instead of making a substantial addition to his friend's bank, he sadly diminished it, which was very far from his friend's thoughts as he gleefully perused the newspaper the following morning. And Thornton maintained to the day of his death that this was the most unlucky week of his unlucky life ; for a good many favourites did win later in the week when he had settled down to field against them, and his weakened bank would not hold out. When the end of the week came, there came with it his usual condition of stony-brokeness ; and once more he carried back to his friend in Birmingham the same old story of his persistent bad luck ; as though luck had anything in the remotest degree to do with the matter.

This betting bout of Thornton's reminds me of a story in which I am not sure he was not one of the actors, although he told the story as a disinterested third party. It concerned his intimate friend, the well-known old Birmingham bruiser, " Fance " Evans, who will be remembered by some of my readers.

After Fance had finished with the ring he became a professional teacher of the " noble art," and as probably no cleverer artiste in his line ever existed he got about him quite a large school, composed of the young swelldom of the place, and I remember he was at the time the principal professor of fistics at the University of Oxford. Among his pupils in Birmingham was a young fellow, the son of a tradesman. Unfortunately the youth had rowdy tendencies, and nothing pleased him so well—especially when he had his mentor with him—as picking a quarrel with some strapping big fellow, and showing off his superior skill. On one occasion, after spending a jolly night together, the professor and pupil were passing through St. Philip's churchyard, homeward, very late at night, when an opportunity, such as the young spark loved, arose. It was a huge fellow belonging to the Corporation night-soil department on the way to his work. At it they went, hammer and tongs, and it was not long before the swell found he had, for once in a way, taken his tools to the wrong shop. The big labourer was knocking him all to smithereens. After the third round he picked himself up with the assistance of Fance, who was acting as his second, while his opponent was waiting quietly at a little distance to see if he required any more.

While Fance was mopping his friend's face, the young man whispered, faintly :

" I've called up the wrong man, Fance. You'll have to lend me one."

Fance got his man up to the scratch for the fourth bout, sticking very closely behind him, apparently to encourage him. Scarcely had they got to work when the labourer caught a terrific blow on the eye, which put the shutter up, and sent him to earth like a stricken ox.

" Take that ! " said the swell, with a chuckle.

" I've got it," said the man, as he slowly raised himself from the ground. " It's too dark to see where it came from ; but it wasn't from the same place as the others, and I don't want any more."

The most widely-known member of our company was, without a doubt, George Luckett, otherwise known as " the Dodger." At that time he was " living on his wits," and a fairly good living they provided him ; he dressed well, ate and drank of the best, and was never short of money. He was one of a sort who did not depend for his success upon such trivialities as luck, or on honest skill even. I have often heard him protest that he did not believe in such a thing as luck. " If you haven't any," he would say, " do as I do, make some. I believe in making my own luck, I do."

But sharp as he was, the Dodger occasionally got taken down. I remember him meeting with an amusing little rebuff at our old tavern. He had found what appeared a very soft thing, a young man who fancied himself at cribbage, and who was, moreover, willing to play for big stakes. You may be sure it was not long before he was owing the Dodger a considerable amount. By and by the seeming " flat " had occasion to leave the room for a minute, and a well-meaning but officious fellow followed him out, and contrived to convey the information to him that he was being done.

" Can't you see," said the informer, " that he's got a pull on you ? And don't you know he is the famous cardsharper, Dodger Luckett ? "

" I don't know, and I don't care. I'm sure my pull is quite as strong as his," was the reply.

" What pull have you ? " asked the other.

" Well, I've got no money, and it's all on the nod."

Mr. Luckett lived to become a big figure on the turf, and as his doings there will aptly illustrate some of the queer, and I may say crooked phases of turf life, I shall have occasion to make him and my readers better acquainted later on.

I must say this for Dodger Luckett; after he had given up cribbage as a profession, and had transferred his remarkable abilities to the betting ring, no temptation of an ordinary kind was powerful enough to get him back to the old game; still, there were times when he was unable to resist a temptation.

I recall a very amusing occasion when he was persuaded to do so—was, in fact, almost bullied into it. We were staying for the Ascot Meeting at an hotel near the course. One evening after dinner an elderly gentleman—an immense swell, evidently by his bearing a military man—entered our room. As he stood just inside the door, bolt upright, I should say six foot three in height, with grey moustache and coloured spectacles, he made a singularly imposing figure.

" Do either of you sporting gentlemen play cribbage ? " he inquired bluntly.

One or two admitted they could play, but were all indisposed to do so just then.

He was standing near Dodger's chair, and laying his hand on his shoulder, he asked if he played. Luckett admitted he did, but he also declined. However, he worried and almost taunted him at last into accepting his challenge. Turning to one of his friends, Dodger whispered :

" It's a nice thing to live to be challenged at my own game by a cove wearing gig-lamps, ain't it ? "

He played and, of course, won every game. The military man declared it was a mere matter of luck ; nothing would convince him he wasn't the better player, and, as a military man ought to be, he was brave, and would have played for heavy stakes if Luckett would have honoured him.   As it was, he lost ten pounds before he could be induced to give in.   It is only fair to the Dodger to say he wouldn't touch a penny of the winnings, but left it towards the hotel bill at the end of the week.

Another member of the motley crew was " Nibler " Birch.   This strange character will only be remembered by the elder race of sportsmen, and among those in the Midlands chiefly, for I think the Nibler seldom travelled far from Birmingham, where he was a very familiar figure from forty to fifty years ago.   He has been so long dead my impressions of him have become weakened, but I distinctly remember there was a good deal of mystery about him and his movements ; nobody seemed to know how he came or went away from anywhere.   Was there a little mill on, or rat-killing, a main of cocks to be fought, or a cribbage match to be played, you would always find Nibler there.   How he got there, or where he went when it was over, nobody ever knew.   Nobody knew whether he was a married man or single, had a home of his own, or was in lodgings ; in fact, how Nibler Birch lived, and where he lived, were two of the mysteries of Birmingham in those days.   Billy Thornton once declared he had come nearer to solving them than anybody else, for he had seen him one night emerge from the dark vaults underneath the Market Hall; perhaps there were stores of hidden treasure there. Another night, or rather early in the morning, after a cribbage match, he had caught sight of Birch flitting like a ghost in the dark, and he determined to find out where he lived, so he tracked him through sundry streets and passages, and finally saw him get over a wall; and that was the nearest anybody ever got to where the Nibler lived.

Birch generally attended the Newmarket meetings, but it always appeared to me not so much for the racing as for the sake of playing hazard. All through the night you could see him sit there right opposite Arthur, the clever old croupier, the mention of whose name will awaken unpleasant memories in some of my readers. I dare say Birch played on a system; most of the frequenters of the table did so. Perhaps that was how he got his money.

Among his other accomplishments, he was a famous bagatelle player, and he used to back himself to hole every ball; and occasionally he had for playfellow Dodger Luckett. On one occasion a friend was betting against Birch doing his great feat of filling all the cups. It happened that the player this afternoon had extraordinary bad luck. He failed in his feat five or six times in succession, and it was not until he had lost his half-sovereign that it occurred to him that it was rather remarkable it was the number three hole he had failed at each

time.   So he rushed quickly to the top of the table, when
lo ! the mystery was explained.   The Dodger had slipped
a small coin in the bottom of number three.

"Ah ! ah ! you've found it out, like all the clever
folks, when your stuff's gone ! " cried Luckett, mockingly.

There came a day when we missed the poor old Nibler.
How he died (if he did die), where he died, or when or
where he was buried, were also mysteries which, as far as
I could learn, nobody ever fathomed.

Neptunas Stagg was not one of our frequent visitors,
being himself the host of a sporting " pub " in Birmingham and, as far as I remember, he never played cards.
I think he came amongst us chiefly because it was the
resort of the principal bookmakers, and probably he
would have a quiet little commission to work for a
future event in racing.   History, however, will hand
down poor old " Nep " as the jockey who steered the
winner of the very first Cesarewitch.   He was a very keen
but much respected man, a peculiar cast in one of his eyes
giving a droll effect to his face, and a certain dry humour,
with a fund of amusing reminiscences, made up a comical
little fellow.   After leaving the public business he became
a member of the old Birmingham Club, which in after
years became the famous resort of Midland sportsmen,
known as the Central Club.   Although but a poor player
at billiards he was extremely fond of the game, and
many a time have I played with him in the dingy old
club-house in Castle Street, which preceded the splendid
building which became the home of sport in Birmingham.

" Nep " married, but had no family. He lived in retirement in one of the suburbs of the town, and it was understood he was not entirely happy in all his domestic relations ; and towards the latter part of his days he became unhinged in his mind. His end was very sad indeed. In the early morning, something more than thirty-three years ago, he was missed from his bed, and his wife, going to seek him, found him head downwards in a rain-water tub, of course dead.

There was another visitor to the old inn whom I have a clear recollection of, and one story of him is worth telling ; this was Bob Brettle, the redoubtable Brummagem boxer. After he had done battle for the championship of England, and had finally retired from the ring, he kept a small public-house very near to the " Coach and Horses," and he frequently joined the merry company there. Some queer stories were told of Bob, but this particular one, which he used to tell of himself, will best deserve repeating. Everybody knows what a lion-hearted fellow the famous bruiser was ; he admitted, however, that he was once in a terrible funk ; and the only time he was thoroughly frightened was while in training, at Hednesford, for his big fight with Mace. Palmer, the murderer, with his friend and victim, Cook, were Brettle's principal backers, and it was his habit to walk over to the old-fashioned country " pub " which was Brettle's quarters, nearly every day. On one of these occasions a great burly navvy was in the tap-room terrorising all the company. Among other dirty tricks he took up glasses and cups belonging to the company, drinking the contents with the greatest insolence. Brettle saw his performance, and it got his blood pretty well up to boiling heat.

"I shall slip into this bully just now," says Brettle; "I can't stand it much longer."

"Don't you be a fool, Bob," said Palmer; "you must not risk getting hurt over such a brute as this. Leave him to me. Now you go yourself to the tap and get a quart of ale, and ask him to have the first drink. He won't refuse."

Brettle was coming through the passage carrying the quart of ale, when Palmer met him, and taking a small paper parcel from his waistcoat pocket, he shook a fine powder over the surface of the ale.

"Now, take it to him, and make him drink first."

This Brettle did, and the navvy almost emptied it at the first pull, and, with scarcely a pause, he put it to his lips again, nearly finishing the lot. For about a quarter of an hour he was noisier than ever; then he became suddenly quiet, and lay down on one of those old-fashioned tap-room settles, and in a minute was fast asleep, the company remarking what a very heavy sleep it appeared; but they thought it better not to disturb him, supposing he would sleep off the effects of the drinking. Toward closing time the landlord began to feel anxious to get rid of him, so gave him a good shaking, without, however, shaking consciousness into him. Brettle, also, becoming now somewhat alarmed, made vigorous but unavailing efforts to arouse him, so they made him a bed of straw in the stable and laid him there.

Brettle had breathed no word of Palmer and the powder incident, but he had a dreadful suspicion, and scarcely slept for thinking of it. His first act next morning was to rush to the stable, where he found the navvy in the same heavy slumber. He administered another dose of shaking, almost pinched a bit out of his ear, and finally gave him a slap on the face with the palm of his hand, which was heard all over the premises, but all without making the slightest impression. As his trainer was waiting for him, Bob was obliged to leave him, but the moment his morning's work was done, full of fear he rushed to the stable again. The navvy lay in the same state he had been in for twenty-four hours. Bob was alarmed now, not only for the life of the brute whom he firmly believed he had been the means of poisoning, but for his own safety. He thought the man was as good as dead—poisoned—and he should be charged with the murder. He wondered whether he had better go to the police-station and give himself up at once, confessing his guilt. He decided against that course, as it would necessitate the implication of his friend, Mr. Palmer. Anyway, he wouldn't do so until he had talked over the matter with that gentleman. He wondered when the inquest would be held—whether the verdict would be murder or manslaughter. Would they put the " darbies " on his wrists when they took him to Stafford Gaol ; and who would be the judge at the next assizes ? He ran through all the great criminal lawyers he had ever heard of, and tried to make up his mind to which he should entrust his defence; and so he worked himself up to a pitiable condition of fear and excitement. During the afternoon he paid numerous visits to the stable. Towards the last the man's heavy breathing had ceased and was only just audible, his huge breast rising and falling like that of a little child. These appearances he took for the certain signs of approaching death. He was horrified and decided to go no more to the stable, but to await in the house, as well as he might, the development of affairs. But the stable had a fascination for him which he was powerless to resist, so once more, before retiring for the night, he took the candle in his trembling hands and again made his way there. One may fancy his amazement when he found the burly form of the navvy had gone. Brettle afterwards said he couldn't, at the time, make up his mind whether the devil or Palmer had stolen the body. He, however, awarded the credit to the latter, after the tragical result of his intimacy with Mr. Cook became known. Bob used to say that it was this episode in the life of the notorious poisoner which first induced suspicion, and which was, therefore, the means of hanging him.

K

CHAPTER X

A Retrospect—Betting and betting men in the sixties: John Jackson, Henry Steel, John Robinson, Richard Henry Fry, the brothers Collins, Sam Wilkinson

IT has been said " adversity makes us acquainted with strange bedfellows " ; it is equally true that an active life on the turf must necessarily make one acquainted with a great variety of characters ; and if one goes about with open eyes, having a faculty for observation, there are opportunities of noting many extraordinary events, as well as strange men ; indeed, I know of no walk in life so fraught with chances for an observant mind as a life on the turf.

Since I commenced these reminiscences of my racing days, how often have I wished I had been blessed with enough wisdom and industry to have taken notes all through my career, with occasional pen-and-ink sketches of the men I have met, and the events I have witnessed during the many years of my turf life. What a mass of valuable material I should have had ready to my hand ; and, instead of the halting and uncertain efforts of memory, I should have been able to reproduce, with life-like accuracy, the actors and scenes of many now forgotten comedies of real life, which would have been interesting to readers of the present generation.

Indulging in a retrospective glance at the turf in the early sixties, and then observing it to-day, what a tremendous change seems to have come over the scene! The whole of what I may call the most important actors on the turf, of those days, have wholly disappeared, actors who afforded us so much profit and pleasure, and alas! occasionally, so much pain. I allude, of course, to the equine celebrities; and how few also of the notable men remain. Owners and trainers of horses, as well as those who backed and those who laid against them, have mostly gone, and a fresh race has taken their places. It is all changed, and methods and habits have altered as much as the people. It was always so, it is inevitable; we that are old become slow, dull of sight, and thick-witted. The young ones arise with keener sight, and generally more vigour, sometimes pushing us from our places, and it would have been well for some of us had we been wise enough to know this is in the everlasting nature of things; we should then have retired profitably, and perhaps gracefully, and not have lingered to be ousted from our places.

As I have already said, the bookmakers of my early days on the turf, as a rule, were not only uneducated but, in language and manners, they were rough and uncouth.

I would not, however, have it assumed that this description applies to all the bookmakers I knew in the sixties. There were notable exceptions; John

Jackson, " Jock o' Fairfield," as he was called, is the first exception I should name. When the decade opened Jackson had been for years the leviathan bettor of the turf, and, quite early in it, his mantle was gradually descending on to the broad shoulders of a more wonderful man.

There is no doubt " Jock " was a bold and ambitious bettor, and withal, an extremely able man. This and a great deal more applies to Henry Steel, who succeeded —if he did not supplant—him as premier fielder and leviathan. Perhaps no man, in any walk of life, ever started to climb the ladder of fortune in all ways more heavily handicapped than Mr. Steel. Despite of this, however, he went rapidly to the front, and ultimately to the very top of his profession.

Nature had endowed him with many of her choicest gifts. He had clear vision and indomitable pluck ; knew what he wanted, and meant to have it. A man of enormous energy, with insight and foresight, and broad grasp of things denoting your really able man, such a one as, with educational and other advantages, might have been fitted to hold the highest places in the State. So one is not surprised that he should become not only a millionaire, but a great commercial magnate.

John Robinson, now " Sir John," who must also be named among these exceptions, was not, I believe, in the circumstances of his early life, so unfortunate as Steel ; but I remember him well when he first appeared on Newmarket Heath in the character of a fielder. His small face, clear cut, and full of character ; his eyes keen as those of a hawk, and his small round head topped with a funny little cap. This was the day of his small beginnings. Observant men, and those who knew him, never doubted he, too, would rise in the world. What he did rise to, and what he is now, with his vast commercial undertakings, are matters of history.

These, then, are the three most notable exceptions to my description of the betting men of the sixties which occur to me at the moment, but there are many more of them, among whom were Sidney Smith, John Foy, Gus Jacobs.

William Collins, my life-long and dear old friend, who after a good many years of quiet and secluded retirement, died at Bournemouth about two years ago.

I have always regretted and shall never cease to regret his fateful invention of the *infallible system*, but I knew he never meant me anything but good; so I have no blame for him. However tragic the invention for me, I alone am blamable for all it did for me. George Collins, a younger brother of my old friend, and for many years my brother's partner, retired from the turf nearly twenty years ago, and has been living an exceedingly quiet life ever since, in the village of Moseley, and in the ancient burying-ground of its beautiful old church—only a few months ago—I, and my brother, with sad hearts, followed him also to his last home. George Collins was a man of the strictest integrity, who won, as he deserved, the respect and confidence of all who knew him. Mr. Edward Collins, in a secluded nook of Branksome Park, Bournemouth, still lives in a feeble condition of health. The brothers Millard, my fellow-townsmen and intimate friends, came on to the turf many years after myself, but they made a great name there, earned by straightforward and honourable dealing. James, the elder, died a few years ago. The popular and genial younger brother retired soon after, but I regret to say in such a sadly broken condition of health; he passed away less than a month ago.

Then there was Richard Henry Fry, a bookmaker and a gentleman, one of the cleverest and best I have met with; tireless and keen, yet as remarkable for his straightforwardness and probity. After many years of intimate acquaintance, I can say I never knew him do an action or say a word unbecoming a gentleman. His most marked characteristic was a boundless generosity—ever ready to help those needing help, he became the victim of a vile conspiracy in his last days, himself needing help, and his end was too sad for words.

I must name with these exceptions my dear old brother, Sam Wilkinson. Of him I need say but little. For many years, in partnership with one or other of the brothers Collins, he did a very large business, and perhaps there was no man among all I have named more respected and more generally beloved.

The large army of noble and gentle backers who were famous or notorious in the sixties I have no space even to mention here. Jacob Bayliss, who came about next after Steel in importance, did not retain his great position to the finish. John Robinson and his brother Sam, whose advent in the ring I so well remember, have " wrapped up " as the saying is, only putting in an occasional appearance, and then only to smoke a well-earned cigar and have a modest flutter for pleasure ; and I am pleased to say they are still in the land of the living. Mr. Sydney Smith, for a good many years before he died, ceased to take any active part as a layer.

I can think of none of the bookmakers of the earlier sixties who have any sort of connection with the ring at the present time. Billy Nicholl, who once bet to a tremendous lot of money, and was accounted a somewhat eccentric individual, lived in retirement at Nottingham for upwards of twenty years, and died there about eleven years ago. Peggy Collins, a sharp, clever fellow, who made a fortune laying against horses, giving way to drink, lost it all again, and came to hanging about outside Tattersall's and other resorts of his old companions, actually begging, and finally finished in the workhouse. The elder Billy Marshall, Sam Houghton, and John Hibbert have been dead many years, but all three of these were represented in the rings for years by sons who played no unimportant part there, and, singularly enough, neither of the three is satisfied with the profession of his sire, but each has combined in his person the character of owner, layer, and backer of horses. It is many years also since Tom Hornsby, Old Stevie, Harry Batten, Keeling and Gibson, Bart Onley, Larry Wallace, Bob Coombes, Turner, of Worcester, Charley Head, Joe Saxon, Tom Manning, George Luckett, and Matt Collinson died ; and in comparatively recent years Jimmy Barber, Joe Slack, John Foy, Waterhouse, Turner Wilson, George Silke, and James O'Connor, and still more recently have Tom Stones, Sydney Smith, and Fry passed away. These were the well-known fielders of the old time. All had done an enormous turn-over, and had been men of wealth and consequence in their time. Many of them retained this position to the end; others, and among them some who in life had been accounted the very keenest and cleverest of all, died in difficulties, nay, in absolute want.

If one could only write a faithful biography of each of these men, what an interesting and startling volume it would make, for mostly they were men with histories behind them.

CHAPTER XI

A wonderful collier—The doll trick—How he opened a banking
account—His first visit to an hotel—Squaring a bad settling
—The collier goes back to the pit—His end

OF all the fielders of this time, excepting the brothers
Collins, the one whom I saw most of, and knew best, and
can best recall, was a very extraordinary character, and
his strange life was made up of more striking vicissitudes
than was that of any of those whose names I have run
through.

This was Dan Lawrence, the famous collier, who came
to the " Coach and Horses " with Mr. Pritchard, and for
the same purpose ; and as he was by far the most extraordinary character who frequented the old house, and
perhaps because I saw more of him, I propose dealing
with him somewhat more fully than I have with the
others ; and, while I am about it, I think it advisable to
carry his story to its sad ending.

When I first knew the collier he was a broad, thick-set,
powerful Black-countryman, who had spent most of his
years underground getting coal ; he had book-learning of
no sort, nor any kind of school education ; he could neither
read nor write, yet his natural intelligence was something

marvellous. Being at a very tender age taken to work down a pit, he had few opportunities of improvement ; but when he became old enough to look about for himself, he soon found out the fact that there was another world beyond the cinder-heaps and pit-banks of his native county ; so he found his way on to the turf and into the betting ring, by what conjunction of strange circumstances I cannot tell ; I only know I found him there, a rough, uncouth, ill-dressed, and ill-conditioned being, a great head on his thick square shoulders, with eyes in it black and piercingly bright, which one soon discovered were capable of seeing whatever was visible to other men, and much also that was hidden from the ordinary ; and his voice, once heard, could never be forgotten. A friend of mine called it something between a policeman's rattle and the roar of a lion. It was truly an awful voice ; I have heard nothing like it, and never expect— and certainly have no desire—ever again to do so.

Well, the collier had not been a member of the ring long before his daring gambling spirit had been rewarded with considerable success.

He was notable for the frequency and good luck with which he played the " doll trick." He, indeed, was the first man whom I can remember practising that dangerous feat ; he would think nothing of laying hundreds of pounds against a hot favourite, and then planking it all down on another horse in the same race. Of course, if you can do this sort of thing successfully, you may soon be rich. The Black-countryman did manage to do it ;

indeed, for two or three years it didn't matter what he did, he could never do wrong; consequently, he had to carry about with him, or stow away somewhere, an amount of ready money which was becoming quite embarrassing. He confided as much to an intimate friend of mine, who thereupon enlightened him upon the subject of banking accounts, recommending him to open one for his own safety and convenience, which he did forthwith, and my friend went with him to the bank for that purpose. He was shown into the banker's parlour, going through the necessary preliminaries, and making some sort of hieroglyphics in a book which was to be taken as his signature, and then he was shown to the counter to make his first deposit, which the banker naturally supposed was going to be merely a few pounds. Fancy the amazement of the bank people when he began to unload himself; producing huge rolls of notes, some of them clean and crisp, on the Bank of England for large amounts, with hundreds of shabby and ragged country-men, looking uncommonly like bits of dirty tobacco paper, but representing altogether many thousands of pounds. It was wonderful where he kept on hauling them from, back and front and all over him; he seemed to have pockets crammed full with the precious paper. I know that within a year or two of opening that account he had no less than £35,000 lying there to his credit. One would think that was a fair share of the commodity for such a man to possess. Evidently he didn't think so, for I have never met with a man more earnest in pursuit of it than he was now ; in fact, the richer he became, the more eager he was for more.

The collier became an owner of racers ; had horses, and trainers, and jockeys, and, who can tell ? perhaps also other human beings with pencils in their nimble fingers, all in his employ, and conspiring to increase his huge pile. He knew nothing of Shakespeare, but an unerring instinct told him—

> " There is a tide in the affairs of man,
>   Which, taken at the flood, leads on to fortune,"

and he had availed himself of that tide, and for a man of his origin and quality he had become inordinately rich. The pity of it was that nobody could drive into his big clever head the meaning of another passage from the great bard about—

> " Vaulting ambition which doth o'erleap itself,"

or he might have been saved from much evil in after years.

Everybody knows that nature has a knack of compensating blind folk for their loss of sight by abnormally developing the sense of touch, or other of the senses ; so it will be found frequently where men cannot write, but are driven to commit to memory what other people commit to paper, that faculty becomes marvellous in its expansion and capability. I have known several cases of this kind, but nothing that equals that of my friend the pitman. His memory was simply wonderful. For several years I shared with him the same private lodgings at the Newmarket meetings and elsewhere, having ample opportunities of proving this statement with regard to his memory. One case I will give my readers illustrative of it, premising, however, that I don't expect every one will be able to swallow the statement entirely; nevertheless it is strictly true.

I may say that the collier had occasionally partners and sometimes clerks, but as a rule he didn't get on well with either; consequently, it was no uncommon occurrence for him to find himself at a race-meeting without either the one or the other. Considering he could not write a single line for himself, it might be supposed that his backing and laying would, on such occasions, be at a standstill. Nothing of the sort; in fact, it seemed to make little difference to him, he would go on with his backing and laying just the same, and when he returned to our lodgings in the evening, and had dined, he would hand his book to me or to one of the others, calling over every bet he had made during the day entirely from memory, where doubtless he had the names of the men and horses, and amounts indelibly impressed, and I do not remember his being at any time convicted of an error. One advantage of this method was such a one as he was peculiarly well able to appreciate; it enable him to dispense with a partner, who would take away some portion of his profits, and to do without a clerk, for whose services he would have to pay.

I will relate one little incident very early in his racing career which will show the utter density of his ignorance regarding the usages of civilised life. Now the pitman's early life, when not underground, had been spent in a dwelling which was more hovel than house, such as was only too common in the pit districts of South Staffordshire sixty years ago. Such a thing as washing themselves upstairs was, of course, unknown. Mostly this service, and other portions of the toilet, were completed in the little living-room, or, as frequently happened, at the pump outside. Fancy, then, our friend's bewilderment the first time he went away from home for a few days, and found himself putting up at a decent hotel. Everything was so strange, so wonderful; carpets on stairs, carpeted rooms, bedsteads with gorgeous hangings, tables with tops of marble, mirrors half as big as himself, chairs with delicate cane seats, and furniture too costly to touch. Coming off a long and dirty journey, he wants to wash and brush up, so " Boots " has carried up his little carpet bag and shown him his bedroom, where he stands motionless, in a puzzled condition, for a quarter of an hour. There is the marble-topped washstand, with soap-boat and large basin, with jug of water, together with all the usual necessaries for a wash, but to the collier these things are strangers. He sees insurmountable obstacles in the way. He looks at the narrow-necked jug, and then at his immense hands, such as pitmen only own, and it was an indisputable fact that they needed washing. But how ? There's the rub. In his perplexity he looks about the room, and seeing a silken cord with a tassel at the end of it, it dawns upon him that this may mean a bell at the other end of it, and as he is not afflicted, even in these early days, with any large amount of timidity,

he snatches at the cord and gives it a tremendous
jerk, so bringing off his first double event—he breaks the
bell-pull and brings up a rosy, good-looking chamber-
maid.

" Cum eer, mi wench," said he. " Wheer bin I to wash
me ? "

" There you are, sir," replied the girl, pointing to the
jug and basin, and looking at the uncouth figure of the
collier with mingled curiosity and alarm. He in his turn
looked with a puzzled expression, first at the girl and
then at the jug, and then at his own huge hands. Turning to her, he asked :

" 'Ow bin I to get mi honds into that jug, wench ? "

This was quite irresistible ; the girl burst into a loud
laugh, and when it subsided she proceeded to separate
the jug from the basin, which the collier had supposed
one article, pouring out the water for him, for which
he showed his gratitude by amatory language and sundry
delicate attentions of a kind so common on the pit-banks
of South Staffordshire fifty years ago.

Before the collier had been long in the ring, by sheer
force of character and boundless audacity he had pushed
himself to the front, and was hobnobbing with dukes,
earls, and all sorts of titled folks, and so fearless was he
about introducing himself to the great ones of the earth,
he didn't draw the line even at royalty itself. On one
occasion a very exalted personage was standing in the
Jockey Club enclosure at Newmarket, within a few yards
of where the collier stood—of course, in the adjoining

enclosure. Royalty intently studying his card, as any ordinary mortal might. Who knows ? perhaps weighing the chances of the runners, and settling it in his own mind which was to carry his bit. The Prince looked up from his card straight into the eyes of the persevering pitman, and the pitman was by no means frightened or abashed ; on the contrary, he leant over the rails in a most familiar manner, and with that indescribable voice of his, roared out :

" Now, then ! W'at wun yer Majesty bok ? "

The genial Prince, with an amused smile, quietly walked away. Doubtless royalty, as well as humble people, may have a flutter occasionally, but it is opposed to the etiquette of royalty to do it directly ; it was always done through the medium of a middleman, generally one of the Prince's intimate friends.

In dress, manners and language, he never was anything but the big pitman, even in his palmiest days. He arrived in Birmingham one night very late—too late, in fact, to get a train to his home on the pit-banks of South Staffordshire. With him was Jem Pritchard, a Black-countryman as unmistakably as was the collier himself. He proposed they should put up till morning at the Queen's Hotel adjoining the station, whither they proceeded. Jem, as I have said, was one of the drollest fellows I have ever met—a real character. He stepped up to the door of the hotel and rang the bell ; then turning to his companion, he whispered :

" Yo' stond back i' the dark, Dan. If the hotel mon

see thy pretty mug, we'll get no lodgin' here; they'll think we bin cum a-cadgin'."

Whenever the collier made one of a party staying and boarding together, he always contrived, if possible, to do the settling. I remember an occasion when the party numbered seven, and we had agreed to pay a guinea each for our beds, and at his request we each paid him our proportion of the bill—including the guineas for beds. The evening we were leaving we left him behind to settle. For some purpose one of the party had to return to the house, and dropped upon the collier haggling with the landlady whether it was guineas or pounds we were to pay for the beds. The poor woman stood but small chance in a bout of words with him, and so we discovered the collier's motive for liking to settle the bills.

The collier was not what is known "as a giver," yet he was not altogether incapable of a generous action, to prove which I may mention an incident arising out of Blue Gown's Derby. He was intimately acquainted with Sir Joseph Hawley, and had large transactions with him. It was a well-known fact that Sir Joseph could never be made to believe that the almost cobby Blue Gown was the equal—much less the superior—of the aristocratic Rosicrucian, and it was also known that this prejudice cost the famous Baronet the trifle of £100,000 or thereabouts. There is no doubt that Sir Joseph had told the collier the whole strength of the business, which had influenced him to lay a considerable sum against Blue Gown, which, of course, he lost and paid. Among his Birmingham

L

friends there was a bookmaker in humble circumstances, to whom—doubtless intending to help him—he gave the tip to lay. At the end of the Derby week he went to see the pitman, and told him that he had so far overlaid his book and crippled his means he should be compelled to pull up lame on the settling day unless he could get help. What was necessary to save him the collier advanced; and more than once, when people have been abusing the collier, I have heard this man stand up for him against all comers, manfully and gratefully defending his absent friend.

In the sixties there was a popular race-meeting in the Isle of Man. It was an agreeable annual outing to Douglas, when a good many of us managed to combine business with pleasure, and it was by no means a little local affair confined to Manxmen and Manx horses; for many of the leading turfites patronised the meeting, and some fairly good horses were sent from England. I recall one occasion when my friend the pitman won a race there. I and my immediate connection being among his supporters we had a jolly time of it; but the return journey took all the jollity out of us.

The Manx boats were not the elegant and comfortable steamers which we see plying between Liverpool and Douglas to-day; the one in which we returned was a wretched old tub, which pitched and rolled about in the most distressing manner. It was bad weather when we started, and we were scarcely clear of the bay when it blew a perfect hurricane, and the face of many a bold

betting man was blanched with fear, and I verily believe
some among them never expected to see their cosy homes
again.   It was one of those occasions which show what
men are made of, and it served to show up the character
of our collier.   It proved his natural cuteness and mother-
wit was more than a match for his better educated
companions.   He actually had the audacity to open an
insurance office, there and then, aboard the steamer.
He began betting £100 to half-a-crown that we got safely
back to Liverpool.   It may seem incredible, but it is true,
that a good many, in the panic of the moment, handed
him their half-crowns for the sake of the long odds, among
the takers being several reputed sharps.   However,
when it dawned upon them that the layer was standing
all these half-crowns to nothing, in spite of sea-sickness
and suffering they were obliged to have a hearty laugh
at each other.

No opportunity of getting a bit ever escaped the
collier. Sagacious and alert, he was always on the
look-out, and nothing missed his keen eyes.   There was
no rule in those days about newly-named horses, or horses
with changed names being advertised to that effect on the
cards.   In this respect there was not the wholesome
protection for innocent backers and layers which this
excellent rule now affords ; consequently at times great
injustice was wrought and much scandal caused.   I
remember one case particularly illustrating this, in which
the collier was concerned.   A horse, known as the Colt by
Trumpeter out of Miss Bowser, won in a canter the first

day of the meeting at Reading. On the following day there was a horse on the card named Hornblower, and when his number went up for the race he was in nobody knew anything about him, and not until the collier had cleared all the market at fives, fours, threes, and even much shorter prices did it become known that this strange horse was the identical Miss Bowser Colt, about which a fair price would have been six to four on, and as he won again, our cute friend must have had a pretty haul.

But cute and clever as he was, there came a day when " vaulting ambition *did* o'erleap itself," and the collier was as incapable of doing right as he had hitherto been incapable of making mistakes ; and it is a fact that when once the tide sets in against a gambler it is all over with him. Having become drunk with success, and full of the egotism born of it, he is sure it will come all right again ; so, with a stubborn faith in his own judgment, he fights fate with a blind valour, and cannot see from whence come the buffets he is getting ; and only when he is panting with distress, utterly and irretrievably defeated, is he able to see the strength of his foe. And then he curses himself for a fool that he had not given up the unequal contest long before, when he might have retired with some honour and credit. So fared it with our clever pitman. His horses went wrong, his jockeys went wrong ; everything went wrong with him. Even the great " doll trick," which he had played so often and with so much success—that also failed him. The pile he had went faster than it came. He had a floorer one week, and he came up smiling the next, with a strong faith in himself, nothing daunted. But now his pluck availed nothing, and fate mocked at his strength and his cunning, and went on to complete his ruin. While this was in progress there were, however, fitful gleams of sunshine for him. I recall, with a vivid distinctness, one week at Newmarket. When the last day of the meeting arrived, he had lost thousands of pounds on the week, and he was making ready to go home, and I never remember him so completely broken down as he then was.

" I'm dun, lads," he said. " I mun goo 'um. You'll never see me i' th' ring again."

It was almost pathetic to see the great, strong fellow at last admitting defeat. Somebody present made the remark that " he might as well be hanged for a sheep as a lamb," and urged him to give it one more trial. He sat with his head in his hands for several minutes, then jumped up, with a look of determination in his eyes ; so he went with us on to the Heath again.

For that day he was once again the wonderful collier. Time after time he laid against the favourite and backed the winner. At the end of the day he had recovered all his losses on the week, and had a balance to the good ; and so for a little time reprieved.

These gleams of sunshine were, however, but transient ; the fickle jade Fortune was merely playing with him. Week after week he continued to lose, until he reached the one preceding the St. Leger, which was a scorcher for him from the first day of it to the last ; and those of us who knew him and his concerns intimately were wondering how he would get over the next settling. Of course, the ring generally knew nothing of the straits the collier was in. Months before this he had backed a horse for the coming Leger for a very large amount, and at this time the horse had come to a short price, and seemed to have a fair chance of winning, so placing him on his feet again. These bets were worth a good deal of money ; so I felt sure that on this account, if the money could by any means be found, the settling would be done. I happened to be lodging at the time with the young man who was acting as clerk to him. The account was made out accurately on the Saturday and posted to the collier, that he might enclose the requisite cheques and forward them on to the agent in London to settle on Monday, and we were left to speculate as to what would come of it. On Sunday morning, to our surprise, the collier himself turned up, looking restless and unhappy. Producing the account he said :

" Look 'ee 'ere, mi lad, this account wunnor do ; I want yo to mak' another."

" What's the matter with it ? " asked the clerk. " It's exactly according to the book."

" Never yo moind the book," replied the collier. " Yo'n left out swells that owe me a heap of money, and there's a neame or two on the t'other side yo can leave out till next week."

Fresh sheets of foolscap, with pen and ink, were provided and carried to the little summer-house at the top of the garden, where the new account, which was to provide a week's grace for the poor collier, was made out and forwarded to London, and being made to show a small balance in his favour, of course no cheque was sent with it. It is unnecessary for me to say there was a good deal of grumbling and dissatisfaction at such an unusual number of mistakes being found in the account, but it was settled as well as possible, and it served to get him over the St. Leger week, and as the horse he had backed won, it was all made right on the following Monday. The account was duly settled, but not without sundry shakings of the head and ominous mutterings of discontent.

Nevertheless, the collier once more enjoyed a passing gleam of sunshine, which was, unfortunately, of short duration. The clouds gathered again above him; so after a little time we missed him altogether—he gave up the fight. The enemy had got him down and kept him there. He returned to his old trade of collier, only not now himself handling the pick and the shovel. With the assistance of, and in partnership with, my old friend William Collins, who had had much dealing with him, he became tenant of several small coal-pits. But even here, in his native regions, an evil fate pursued him: instead of a coal-pit it seemed he had leased an underground reservoir, and in place of coal they hauled up little but water; so the undertaking failed, and the friend who had helped him lost several thousands of pounds by it.

He tried the public-house, and that looked like providing

him with a living, and quite as much of luxury as he had allowed himself in his richest days. I cannot tell how it came about, but after a while this also failed him, and he became really very poor. I am told worse than poor—old, and terribly afflicted with an incurable malady—he passed away, after many years of weakness, and suffering, and poverty. Few would have recognised in the broken and decayed old man the strong, clever, and rich collier of forty years ago.

CHAPTER XII

A penitential mood—The prayer of an apostate—A Band of Hope meeting—" The broken heart "

LET no one imagine that in the midst of this whirl of racing, gambling, and drink, I was always and entirely happy. At the risk of being laughed at by some of my friends, I am going to confess I was not. Deep down in my heart were feelings undreamt of, and perhaps not understandable by my companions—a sense of remorse and unrest, a feeling that I was not meant to go by this way, but by a widely different one.

During what I must call the religious period of my life, I had had lapses which pained my friends, and gave me uncomfortable days and nights. These lapses originated, I believe, in a study of Voltaire, Rousseau, Tom Paine, and others of the like, whom I found Paley and Simpson powerless to counteract; but I had never before gone wholly and openly over to the enemy, and I was troubled with many doubts as to the wisdom of the course I had taken; and, at times, an overpowering force seemed driving me back to the old ways.

During one of these religious backslidings the verses inserted here were written, and I beg my critical reader to believe I print them now with no purpose of showing my poetical wares, but with a simple desire to give just a glimpse of my mind during the time I was struggling with influences so opposite.

The Prayer of an Apostate

Friend of the poor and sad ! bend low Thine ear ;
　A heavy sorrow is upon me now ;
My eyes, for aye, refuse the kindly tear,
　And clouds have chased the sunbeams from my brow,
And human hopes, erstwhile so bright and clear,
　Dear God ! are gone—ah, dead for ever now !

Bend, bend Thine ear ; come to me once again !
　To-night great sorrow hath crushed all my pride ;
I turn to Thee in darkness and in pain ;
　The fount of human love for me is dried,
And ev'ry human sympathy is vain,
　And none can help, if Thy help be denied.

Then come, oh, come ! my bruised heart doth yearn
　To feel Thy Spirit move in me once more ;
Rekindle here Thy fires, and let them burn
　But once again, as in the days of yore.
I feel Thou wilt, I know Thou could'st not spurn
　The humbly penitent from mercy's door.

These verses, and the rather gloomy matter which opens the chapter, having worked me into a penitential mood, I may as well make one or two other confessions, and have done with it.

For years after I became a professional racing man I found it impossible to go into any place of worship. Such a coward was I in these matters the solemn tones of a church organ, heard in the distance, or a familiar hymn-tune on a hurdy-gurdy in the street, would make me run away. And yet at times I yearned, with a yearning almost irresistible, to go back to the other life, and sit once more among my old friends.

I remember a night when I was making my way to a rendezvous of sport in Birmingham, I had to pass a small meeting-house with which, in other days, I was well acquainted; and where, had I dared to put my head inside, I should have been instantly recognised. The room was lighted up, and a meeting of some sort in progress. The sound of sweet voices singing a glee arrested my footsteps, nor for the life of me could I move from the spot while the sounds continued. When they ceased I felt impelled to go inside; so crept stealthily into the little vestibule, and listened to a young man pleading with youngsters to avoid the temptations of drink. It was a " Band of Hope " meeting. I heard the whole of the little speech, and then the chairman called upon another young man for the next item on the pro-gramme. This was a recitation, popular at such meetings in those days, and it may be so now for aught I know; it was called " The Broken Heart." Before the reciter had got through half-a-dozen lines I rushed half-mad from my hiding-place. I could bear it no longer, and, as quickly as possible, I was in the midst of my new friends, with a pack of cards in my hands, trying to forget all about it. " The Broken Heart " was a poem I had written several years before; the teetotallers had it published, and it became popular among them as a recitation. It is not so long ago I received the original

MS. of this very poem from Mr. Edward Pickering, Mayor of Durban and a wealthy colonial merchant, who, as a young man and a teetotaller, had been entrusted with the printing of it in Birmingham more than fifty years ago. In the letter which accompanied it, Mr. Pickering hoped that the sight of this soiled and time-worn manuscript would awaken some pleasant memories, assuring me, at the same time, that the piece had been of much service in South Africa. Alas! alas! what pleasant thoughts could it—or anything like it—produce for me?

On another occasion I was with my brother in Liverpool, awaiting the races at Aintree. I had seen an announcement on the hoardings in the town that the celebrated preacher, Charles Vince, of Birmingham, would lecture in some institute or hall there. After dinner, I said to my brother:

" The Reverend Charley is lecturing in Liverpool to-night, and I should so like to hear him again, if one might hear and see him and not be seen."

"Oh, that is easy enough!" replied Sam; "we will go."

In good time, before the lecture commenced, we made for the hall, paid for seats on the floor, and had time to secure them not far from the platform, where we could see and hear our old friend. If I remember rightly, in the shade of a gallery, or screened from his keen eyes by a friendly pillar, we were both interested and delighted with the lecture, and also with the success of our arrangements for avoiding the lecturer. We had turned to leave the hall, when we were stopped by the sound of a well-remembered voice :

" Hi ! hi ! you chaps there ! Are you going to turn your backs on an old friend in that way ? " and down from the platform stepped the Rev. Charles, his face still ablaze with the old genial smile.

Well, having unbosomed myself of these confessions of little weaknesses, as some of my readers, maybe, will deem them, I must get along with my life on the turf, wherein I shall have to introduce many scenes and characters of quite another sort ; as well as reminiscences of some of the principal race meetings, with which I was so familiar for many years.

CHAPTER XIII

Newmarket in old times—Newmarket in the sixties—Backing a winner after the number was up—A struggle for a big stake—Warwick races—A dust up with thieves—What came of it

FOR more than 250 years Newmarket has been the acknowledged headquarters of horse-racing in this country, and during nearly the whole of that time it has been the resort of all the noblest and best in the land, and more or less under the patronage of royalty itself. The pedantic Scotchman, James I., whatever his faults, was an earnest supporter of the sport, and must have the credit of being the first kingly patron of Newmarket. The reign of his unfortunate son, the first Charles, was too full of trouble to allow him time for this or any other kind of sport, and of course the Puritans of the Commonwealth could not be expected to have any leaning that way; and yet there is ample evidence that even old " Noll " was a dear lover of good horses, and went so far in encouragement of their breeding as to keep thorough-breds himself.

That merry gentleman, Charles II., in the matter of horse-racing made, however, full amends for the short-comings of the Commonwealth and his father's unhappy reign ; he not only revived all the glories of Newmarket but he lifted it to a prouder pre-eminence than it had ever possessed ; which position it has held unchallenged down to the present day. Charles built stables there, the remains of which have been visible in our time ; he kept an important stud of racers, attended most of the meetings, and in fact lived no inconsiderable portion of his time in the quaint little Cambridgeshire town. The most important races hitherto had been run over what was known as " The Bell Courses," and the most valuable prizes had been bells. These he discontinued, and introduced cups, or bowls, on which were engraved the pedigree and exploits of the winners. And while, all over the country, he did his best to foster and encourage the popular sport, it was Newmarket that chiefly benefited by his patronage ; and there its influence remained a power for generations. William III. was extremely fond of racing, founding an academy for riding, and gave a number of plates to be run for.

Queen Anne followed in the footsteps of our Dutch king, and, by her constant presence and encouragement, did much to strengthen the hold which racing had obtained on the habits and affections of the English people. George I. was not behind either of his immediate predecessors in this respect. He abolished plates, and gave instead what was then considered of much more value and importance—prizes of 100 guineas each.

George II. also patronised horse-racing, and in the thirteenth year of his reign secured the passing of an Act of Parliament for its better regulation. In the first place he suppressed pony-racing, and, in fact, forbade all weak and under-sized horses of all sorts engaging in the sport; and no race was to be of less value than £50, a penalty of £200 being imposed on the owner of every horse competing in such race, and £100 for anybody guilty of publicly advertising it. Another drastic change was that no person should enter more than one horse for any stake, nor run any horse not bona-fide his own property; and the penalty for breach of this part of the new law was the forfeiture of the horses entered or running contrary to the Act.

Of course, no such thing as handicapping was known in those times, and, in the light of our experience, our ancestors' notions of weight-for-age conditions appear simply ludicrous. The Act says that five-year-olds shall carry 10 stone; six-years-olds, 11 stone; and seven-year-olds, 12 stone each. They knew nothing in those times of two-year-old five-furlong sprints, which in our time form so large a part of every race programme, and which are, in the opinion of some of the authorities, steadily working a deterioration in the quality of our thoroughbreds.

The two courses at Newmarket in the days of which I have been writing were known as the " Long Course," 4 miles 380 yards, and the " Round Course," which was 6,640 yards, or only 780 yards less than the Long Course. Childers—then supposed to be the fastest horse ever foaled—is said to have done the former in $7\frac{1}{2}$ minutes and the latter in 6 minutes 40 seconds; but, of course, it is open to question whether our great-grandfathers had the same perfect means of timing races which exist at the present day.

Newmarket and its doings having for so many years engaged my thoughts, and occupied my time beyond every other resort of the racing man, and loving the dear old town and its breezy Heath, must be my excuse for this rather long digression into its ancient history. In the times of which I am now to treat, some of the meetings began Monday morning and finished the following Saturday afternoon. It was inconvenient, if not impossible, to get from Birmingham to Newmarket on the Sunday, consequently I and my friends had to get to Cambridge by the first train Monday morning, and from thence, hiring horses and vehicles, drive like mad to catch the first race. Our party, as a rule, consisted of my brother, the two elder Collinses, and myself. Ned Collins, having been a Brummagen butcher boy, had acquired the secret of getting out of the gee-gee all its possibilities in the matter of speed, so on these occasions he used to insist on holding " the ribbons," with a result which, I fear, was by no means agreeable either to the horse or its owner, but he generally managed to get us on to the Heath before the numbers were hoisted for the first race.

Newmarket, in the days of my earliest recollections of it, retained many of its ancient characteristics, and amongst its habitués it was easy to see old English noblemen and squires, whose quaint dress and manners left no

M

doubt about their being survivals of a past age. In the shape of enclosures, grand stands, or shelter of any kind, there was little accommodation on any part of the Heath ; nor did we feel very greatly to need them. Numbers of ladies and gentlemen rode about the Heath, while most of the others came in carriages. Even the professional betting men hired carriages of some sort or brought their own, and very largely the betting was done from these carriages, driven to the various finishing posts, and drawn up by the side of the course. This was long anterior to the inventions of " Tattersall's Enclosures," and the one or two small rings then in existence were comparatively little used for betting purposes, for the reason that the winning-posts were all over the Heath, and sometimes at a considerable distance from either of these small enclosures ; and when it was drawing near the time for the decision of a race, nearly everybody hurried off, helter-skelter, with carriages, hacks, and on foot, to see the finish, and to bet to the last moment.

As through the vista of nearly fifty years all these scenes crowd upon my memory, it is strange how vividly some incidents—trifling enough in themselves—rush into my memory. One of my very early recollections of Newmarket is associated with two old northerners, who, in their different lines, were among the greatest men the turf has produced. There is at this moment an incident concerning these two men in my mind's eye as vividly impressed as if it were quite a recent event. On the Heath a great number of carriages are congregated near one of the many winning-posts; for, as I have elsewhere observed, in those days there was but scant accommodation for race-seeing, or betting on grand stands and enclosures; hence the tops of these carriages were used for those purposes. I see, standing on the roof of one of these broughams, a man with a pair of field-glasses held to his eyes, eagerly scanning a crowd of gallant horses as they fly across that noble course, while, ever and anon, his stentorian voice is heard above the clamour of the crowd, now shouting for one horse, and then against another. He appears to me a most excitable man, at the moment worked up to the highest pitch. He is stepping backwards and forwards on the top of the carriage, making every moment some tremendous bets. This is John Jackson, the leviathan bookmaker, who, for a second, seems perilously near stepping backwards off the top of the carriage, which means probably a broken back or a broken neck.

A genial old gentlemen, seated on the driving-box of the next carriage, sees the danger, and as the great fielder, forgetting everything in his intense excitement, is stepping back once more, this time on the very outmost edge of the roof, he cries out:

" For God's sake, be careful, John, or you'll break your neck! " and I think it is not unlikely that the old man's timely warning saved Jackson's life. That quaint old gentleman was John Scott.

The practice of rushing away to see the race sometimes resulted in extraordinary *contretemps*, and more than once I have known the few bookies and backers remaining in the ring go on with their betting sometimes after the race was over, quite oblivious of the fact.

There was, I remember, a little betting ring near the spot where some years ago the principal grand stand was erected. From this place there was but scant opportunity of seeing anything of the racing.

At the single entrance stood a movable pay office, something like a sentry box. Now it must be remembered I am speaking of my first visit to the classic Heath, my knowledge of racing matters and racing men being of the most primitive description. Along with me was Mr. W. Collins, afterwards to become widely and more familiarly known as " Spectacle Collins," He was the eldest of that ilk ; he was then, however, just as green as myself.

The numbers were hoisted for a match, a regular gamb-ling affair, between Money Spinner and a horse named Catalogue, belonging to the hapless young punter, the Marquis of Hastings.

It was a near thing between them " on form," so that the betting was extensive and furious. I had no interest in it, but thought I should like to see the race, which was quite impossible while standing in the ring, the winning-post being nearly a quarter of a mile away, so I mounted the rails and held myself up by the top of the sentry-box. I was scarcely there when I saw the race was actually being run, indeed, was nearly over.

" Why, Catalogue wins," I said to Collins, who stood below me.

" What's that you say ? " inquired a sagacious-looking gentlemen, who, at that very moment, was passing into the ring.

" Catalogue has won now," I repeated.

Instantly the sagacious one rushed into the ring, and from my coign of vantage I saw him, book in hand, popping from one to another of the fielders, and I should say he would have made quite a number of bets before it was known the race was over ; for before the people in the ring were aware the horses had started the winner's number went up. And this was by no means the first time—or the last—that such a thing has been known to happen at Newmarket.

One of the Newmarket races which has left its impression on my mind belongs to this time, and it was one also in which the Marquis of Hastings was interested. I often think the memories of our old jockeys must be stored with endless pictures of great races which have become historical.

I wonder whether Tom Cannon or Charley Maidment— both jockeys who have played a notable part in the great races of the past, and both happily remaining with us to-day—ever think of that fierce fight of theirs for the Cambridgeshire of 1864. I witnessed it, and can see it now " in the mind's eye." I had been stalled off Ackworth by old Dan Lawrence, and rushed on to Lord Stamford's Brick, who was about second favourite, and I was not long kept in suspense about him, for a long way on the other side of the winning-post there were only two in it ;

they were the Marquis of Hastings' Ackworth, with Cannon in the saddle, and Baron Rothschild's Tomato, Maidment up. They were both three-year-olds, carrying 7 stone and 7 stone 5 pounds respectively. Ackworth had been beaten less than a length for the Cesarewitch in a tremendous field of twenty-nine, and although there were four or five better favourites for the Cambridgeshire, he had a strong following. On the other hand, Tomato was one of the most despised of the whole party, and really had no price at all. Both jockeys were extremely good lads, just beginning to give promise of the brilliant future that lay before them. I always thought Maidment, as a lad, looked rather delicate, and there is no doubt he was, and owing to that fact the layers missed, by the merest shave, what would have been one of the most perfect "turn ups" ever known in racing. As I have said, a long way from home the well-known scarlet and white hoops of the Marquis and the bonnie blue jacket and yellow cap of the good old Baron were right bang in front, and we knew the final struggle would be with them.

And what a struggle it was! As they neared the goal the lads went at it hammer and tongs, riding as for dear life, and putting in every atom they possessed. The noble animals, inspired, as it seemed, by the same spirit, exerted themselves to the utmost and answered bravely every call. Now the horse seemed having a shade the best of it, and now the mare ; head and head together they came along, and as amid intense excitement they so passed the post, the bookies screamed loudly for the Baron, and the followers of the Marquis for his horse, while many thought it was a dead heat, and only " the man in the box " could tell that Ackworth had landed by the shortest of heads.

Warwick, after Newmarket, was my favourite race meeting, and I could tell of many ups and downs there, but I shall relate only one tragic episode which resulted in my being once more a broker.

Warwick may be classed among the ancient English race meetings, and, like other of these old-fashioned affairs, it has been the subject of many " ups and downs." In the eighteenth century and during the early years of the nineteenth it enjoyed great consideration, and was a resort of all the prime old sports among our fathers and grandfathers. Of course, the racing was an altogether different thing from that which exists in the present day, when a programme is made up almost entirely of five furlong races, and the majority of the performers are perhaps two-year-old horses. Then the runners were nearly always four-year-olds and upwards, which is natural when we come to consider that such a thing as handicapping was unknown ; the courses were generally from two to four miles, and as the races were nearly all run in heats, it was not unusual for a horse, carrying much heavier weights than those allotted at the present time, to have to do sixteen miles before being proclaimed the winner, and generally he would have to travel twelve miles. Hence it happened that, as a rule, the race-card —if such a thing was then known—would only contain two or three items. At Warwick it was quite the proper thing for the pauses between the various heats to be occupied by a little cock-fighting, or a merry mill between a couple of Brummagem boys.

Coming nearer to our own times, and well within the memory of some among us, I may mention that as far back as the September meeting, 1842, there were evident signs of a decadence in this good old meeting, and one sporting writer of the day bewails the fact in most plaintive language, contrasting the miserable acceptance of six for its glorious old Gold Cup—which, by the by, was won that year by the famous old jockey, Sam Darling, grandfather of the eminent trainer of our day, bearing the same name, on Mr. Holme's Vulcan—with that of 1830, when there were thirty-one subscribers, many of them horses of the highest class, and when the trophy was captured by that real good horse, Birmingham, who won the Leger the following week. Through the forties and fifties there was, I am afraid, still a downward tendency. The swells of the county had largely withdrawn their patronage and at one time there looked like being a collapse.

It was Warwick in the sixties, however, that I was almost intimately acquainted with, and during that decade I saw some splendid sport there, and meetings which were a credit to the old place. A better spirit pervaded the local gentry, and the swells among the owners began again to look with favour upon the meeting, and consequently many of the equine cracks of the time were to be found there. I have a perfect recollection of some of these, and the races they figured in ; but perhaps the one race of that time which clings to my memory most tenaciously was a very small and unimportant affair at the September meeting in 1865. But before I come to this race I must relate a little adventure of the previous week.

I was at Lichfield Races, and had remained on the course till after all the people had returned to the city, for the purpose of seeing a horse I was interested in having a " rough up " with one which had been running during the day, and it was after six o'clock when, all alone, I set my face towards the city. Although it was more than a couple of miles to my destination, it was at that time my custom to walk down from the course, as I had many times witnessed the dangers attending the drive down in the wretched old conveyances which were pressed into this service on these occasions. I left the turnpike road and went by the back lanes, and was strolling leisurely along when, suddenly making a bend in the road, I came upon a scene which quickened my movements. A hundred yards in front of me I beheld a couple of powerful young ruffians seize a slim, well-dressed young man with the evident intention of " running the rule over him," and there is no doubt that but for my opportune arrival he would have had a rough time of it. The first intimation the ruffians had of the presence of a fourth party was when one of them got a tremendous whack from a strong cudgel I carried in my hand. The first effect of this was to liberate the young man, and then the thieves, seeing there were two to two and one tolerably well armed, took to their heels and were soon out of sight.

" You had a near shave of being turned up, sir," I said, recognising in the young man a youthful recruit to the turf, who afterwards became an important figure upon it.

" I had, indeed," he replied, " and I thank you for your timely assistance."

The upshot of it was that we walked back to the city together, and over a bottle, at the " Swan," he became very confidential about certain horses he was going to buy, and hoped he might be able to repay me for the services I had rendered him.

Just as we were about to part, taking hold of my hand, he said :

" I should like to do you a good turn, old fellow, and I think I know a real cert for a race at Warwick next week. You saw old Wynnstay run second for the Cup to-day ? "

" Yes, of course, I have seen that."

" Well, take no notice of that," he resumed ; " but look out for him in a race at Warwick, and don't speak of it to anybody."

I knew my young friend was in a position to know more about it than I could, and I had the strongest reasons for believing he would do me a turn if he could, so I was on the watch for old Wynnstay the following week. I discovered him in a little handicap—I think only a paltry fifty-pound plate the first day. When the number board was hoisted I found there were only five runners, and I made them out a very bad lot, and although

Wynnstay was at that time no flyer, and had not, I believe, won a single race during the season, he appeared to have nothing to beat here. Handley rode him and Fred Webb rode Muezzin, and I must confess that I would have felt much more easy in my mind if the jockeys had been reversed. Well, the betting was 3 to 1 on the field, and at about this price the two I have named and one called Citron were backed furiously, while Distaff and Rhine Wine were also fancied. I had already backed the old horse for as much as I could well afford, and was about going on to the stand to see the race when I saw my young friend, book and pencil in hand, very busy taking all the 5's to 2 he could get Wynnstay.

" Have you backed him ? " he asked quietly.

" I have," I replied.

" Well, don't be afraid," he rejoined ; " he will win easily."

At this I returned to my bookies and put down a considerable amount more, and did not reach the stand till the horses were on the way home. I was dreadfully nervous, because I knew I had bet more than I ought on one race, and if it went against me it would pretty well break me once more. The first good look I got of the race I could see that Wynnstay and Muezzin had slipped away from the field and were coming on by themselves, and the excited partisans of each all around me were shouting themselves hoarse ; I could not shout, the tension of my mind was too great for that. I could only stare straight at these two horses and the two lads on their backs, each making superhuman efforts to get in front, and neither seemed able to do it.   I felt cold at the heart, and was conscious of turning all sorts of colours ; it was quickly over, and I was out of one trouble to be in another. Muezzin, they said, had won by a short head ; I could not have known that if I had not seen the fatal number go up.   This, then, was the result of that young man's genuine desire to help me, and this was the reward of my good action on his behalf in the lonely Lichfield lane. I had lost all my money, and should be a cripple, pecuniarily, for some time to come.   But I lived to laugh at my folly in having so many eggs in one basket, and a long life, with perhaps more than a fair share of life's vicissitudes, has taught me that we cannot always tell which are our blessings and which our curses.

CHAPTER XIV

Stockbridge in old times—In the sixties—A sensational race—
An expensive dinner

DURING my early struggles I was so many times reduced
to a condition of having to begin the game all over again
that I had now got quite used to it. Somehow, however,
I always managed to scramble out of my difficulties, and
get a new start, as I did on the present occasion. I was
a long time reaching anything like a substantial position ;
but, in spite of my many deviations from the paths of
true bookmaking I did ultimately achieve a considerable
success, and for very many years occupied a fair position
in the ring, travelling to every part of the country,
attending race-meetings of every description in pursuit
of my business as a bookmaker.

The chapters which follow are reminiscences of those
years. Unfortunately, I took no notes as I went along ;
had I done so, I have no doubt that these rambling stories
of an old racing man would have been worth reading.

A good many of the old race meetings, to which I
travelled regularly once a year, have disappeared altogether, and their places have been taken by huge company concerns ; race meetings with expensive clubs ;

gates here and gates there; with rings of all sorts, with charges of admission to them all, ranging from one shilling to fifty times as much for a single day's racing. This will, of course, mean an improvement in some respects, at a tremendously increased cost to the regular race-goer but with big dividends to the happy holder of shares.

After all, I look back regretfully to those old open race-courses which have gone for ever. I know they had their objectionable features; but had they not compensating qualities?

Of all the lost meetings none has left such a void as Stockbridge; none was of such antiquity and importance, and to not one of them does memory cling with such strength and tenderness.

Stockbridge, after a long and, taking it altogether, most successful career, came to an end more than ten years ago, and many of the elder members of the racing world will regret exceedingly the old Hampshire meeting. For them there are few race-courses around which gather such pleasant memories; excepting Newmarket, I don't know of any. In the early days of my racing life I remember how eagerly I anticipated the Hampshire week. It was not only that the racing was so high-class and enjoyable, but the whole surroundings of the meeting were pervaded by a spirit of quiet orderliness and dignified repose. You got lots of things here which were pleasant to have, and rarely obtainable elsewhere; while many of the most objectionable features of racing at nearly all other places were entirely absent.

I stayed at the pleasant little market town of Andover for many years during the race week, and not the least of its pleasures was the delightful drive every morning over that lovely stretch of country which lies between Andover and the Grand Stand at Stockbridge; enlivened, as the drive invariably was, by puns, and jokes, and racy stories, accompanied by the best of cheer and the presence of dear old friends who, alas! are dead or scattered—gone beyond the possibility of reviving these happy days here or elsewhere.

A glance through the scanty racing chronicles of the eighteenth century, although they fail to tell us much we should like to know, cannot fail to amuse us; but the one thing which impresses us beyond everything else is the tremendous change which has been wrought not only in the appearance, habits, and spirit of sportsmen, and in the surroundings of sport, but in the nature and condition of the sport itself. There were no handicaps such as we know. The only handicaps our forefathers knew anything of was a system of giving horses with the longest legs the most to carry; or, what they called, "weight for inches," so that any one possessing a good little one had a fair chance of clearing the board. Then they knew nothing of five furlong races; indeed, there were rarely any under two miles, and most of them were four, and run, be it remembered, in heats; so that it would frequently happen that the winner would have to win four races.

Betting was carried on altogether differently to what it is in these days; although there was plenty of it, there were no loud-voiced bookmakers, whose profession it was to lay against all runners. It must not be imagined that because the exigencies of racing had not yet called into existence this professional element that therefore there was no scope for the ingenuity and perseverance of the sharper, a creature not peculiar to racing, or indeed to any form of sport, but who will be found in every profession, class, and condition of human life. It has always seemed to me that the old practice of running races in heats lent itself in a remarkable way to " roping," and other fraudulent practices, and one can but smile as we read such meagre accounts of the betting as are handed down to us. In 1775, Stockbridge and Bibury Club had three days, and, including a match, they had five races on the three days. But frequently one race was enough for the day, especially where there were four heats of four miles each, with an hour perhaps between the heats, this time being usually occupied as at Warwick with fighting a main or two of cocks, a bout of fisticuffs, or other sport. In one of the races on the last day of the meeting there were four runners. Before the start a very short price was taken about Mignonne, who was the public favourite. She won the first heat very easily, and one would think that should have made her still a better favourite for the race, but that was not so ; indeed, she was ousted altogether, and Miss Bell, who could only just manage to get fourth in the first heat, was not only a better favourite, but she improved so much, in less than an hour, that she very easily disposed of Mignonne and the others in the remaining two heats. It is wonderful how often the winner of the first heat, although meeting his opponents over the same distance and on exactly the same terms, is nowhere in the succeeding heats, and it appears a bit suspicious to us moderns. I notice a race where Mr. Medley's Bacchus was thought real jam, and odds of six to four were laid on his beating his solitary opponent. He won the first heat so easily that the odds lengthened to seven to one on him, but his opponent, the Duke of Cumberland's Ora, won the second heat just as easily, and for the final heat seven to one was laid on the Duke. So if there had only been anybody knowing enough to systematically take odds, what a good thing they might have made of it, but gentlemen then only betted with each other.

The Duke of Bolton and His Royal Highness of Cumberland, during the seventies of the eighteenth century, seem to have been great supporters of Stockbridge, and Bibury Club. The latter, who kept an immense stud of horses in training, usually had one or more entered in all the races, and he won with a good many of them. Toward the end of the century, and in the early years of the nineteenth, the Prince of Wales had taken the place of the Duke of Cumberland, and kept an even larger stud. And as he was a constant patron, Stockbridge became, at this time, one of the most fashionable meetings in the whole list, and it was doubtless a brave sight to see the meeting of the Club, composed not of the swelldom of a county only, but of all the young bloods of the country ; with the first gentleman of Europe, the Prince Regent,

N

at their head, in the uniform of this aristocratic Club, green coats, buckskin breeches, and top-boots.

For a good many years after the Regency, the meeting, which had fallen on bad times, remained in low water, and much of the credit of its revival belongs to John Day, who, in the early sixties, took charge of it, providing special accommodation for the many noble patrons at Danebury, and for the aristocracy generally; and never, perhaps, in its long history had it seen such glorious times as those of the sixties. And these were the times I knew it best, and looking back to them, memory is crowded with faces and forms and stirring incidents which the space at my disposal will not permit me to reproduce. Among the owners I was in the habit of seeing there were the Dukes of Beaufort, St. Albans, and Hamilton; Lords Portsmouth, Uxbridge, Ailesbury, Stamford, Westmorland, Vivian, Falmouth, and the unfortunate young Hastings; Baron Rothschild, Sir Joseph Hawley, Sir Frederick Johnstone, Sir William Throckmorton, Count Lagrange, Mr. Merry, Mr. Cartwright, Mr. Chaplin, Mr. Ten Broeck, good old George Payne, and a host of others. Of this long list only two are living to-day, Mr. Chaplin and Sir Frederick Johnstone. The most prominent among the gentlemen riders—and this was ever a great meeting for them—were Captains Little, Knox, Scobel and Coventry; Messrs. W. Bevill, Edwards, and G. S. Thompson. The chief professionals whom I remember there were Fordham, Daley, Wells, A. Day, Custance, Arthur Edwards, Aldcroft, Rogers,

Tom French, Chaloner, the two Grimshaws, the three Adams, and Tom Cannon. The latter, destined to become more intimately associated with the place than either of the others, made his first appearance there Thursday, June 23, 1864, and my old friend, Teddy Brayley, gave him the first mount where he was afterwards to achieve so much glory. The horse was a three-year-old called Black Friar, 6 stone 12 pounds, which weight, however, he was not quite able to do, and consequently had to put up one pound extra. He was unbacked and ran nowhere. The following day, in a big field of eighteen, he rode The Star, 6 stone 13 pounds, and managed to get a good third to Sam Adams on a colt by Vedette, who beat Fordham on Missionary, after a magnificent race, by a head. These were the only two mounts the future master of Danebury had at the meeting that year. The following year we find him doing better in the matter of mounts, riding for Brayley again, for Lord Hastings and others, but with no win, and although he rode regularly he won very few races here for several years, and it was not until 1870 that he made any mark at Stockbridge; then he won five out of fourteen mounts.

One of the most brilliant of all the Stockbridge meetings of my time was that of 1866. It was not only made glorious by a great company of the cream of English aristocracy—male and female—and all our most distinguished professional and gentlemen riders, but also by the presence of an unusual number of equine celebrities.

Two notable youngsters—Hermit and Marksman— first and second in the Derby of the following year— made their appearance on the scene ; but without being in opposition, both ran twice at the meeting, and both were victorious each time.

For the principal two-year-old race there was a grand field, numbering no less than sixteen. In spite of this, however, odds were laid on Mr. Chaplin's gallant little chestnut, Hermit. Pericles and Veridis had lots of admirers. Fordham donned the light blue and white hoops of the Duke of Beaufort on Vauban, and, in my mind's eye, I can see him and his horse, and the determined face of Harry Custance, and the brave little chestnut, fighting out the battle between them, as vividly and clearly as it were yesterday. Hermit had the best of it by a neck, which, singularly enough, was the exact distance he beat Marksman for the Derby, on which occasion Vauban was third.

What I said of the previous meeting might be repeated respecting that of 1867. I saw Lord Hastings' beautiful two-year-old filly, Lady Elizabeth, one of the best he ever owned, canter away from Ironmaster and The Earl for the Eltham Plate. The Marquis owned the Earl also, and, declaring to win the mare, extremely long odds were laid on her. Fordham rode the winner, Tom Chaloner the second, and Tom Cannon, The Earl, who finished a long way in the rear, although, no doubt, Cannon, if he would, could enlighten us a good deal on that matter ! For myself, I have not the slightest doubt he could have finished close up with his stable-companion if there had been any need for it, for it is absolutely certain he was a ton in front of Ironmaster, even if he was not better than Lady Elizabeth, which has always been a matter of controversy.

Later on we saw Lord Lyon, then a four-year-old, with Chaloner in the saddle, give a year and 6 pounds and a beating to that good old horse, Ostreger, with Fordham up, a two-year-old of Lord Hastings—Mameluke, Sammy Kenyon—being a bad third.

The Cup of 1868 was not a very exciting affair. The betting indicated the good thing it was for Knight of the Garter—just then at his best—to beat that great mare, Achievement, who had deteriorated very much from her form as a two or a three-year-old. Now she could not even beat Mr. Saville's two-year-old, Ryshworth. Much more exciting was that magnificent struggle for the Troy Stakes, the following day, when John Daley on Ryshworth, Fordham on Belladrum, and Custance on Mr. Chaplin's Orphan, made one of those finishes which live in the memory for ever.

They went past the post in the order named, all these three consummate artistes, pulling out every ounce that was in them, and at the finish nobody knew, excepting the judge, that Daley had just pipped them.

But talking about sensational races, that for the Hurstbourne Cup beats all. There were but three runners; and one of those, Mr. J. B. Morris's Birdseeker, I may dismiss at once by saying he had not a million to one chance, and was never able to go the pace with the other two.

They were both denizens of one stable, and owned by a most noble duke; their names, in short, were Julius and Gomera. Everybody knew, of course, that Julius was a very long way in front of the mare, so much so, there was no need to make any declaration. It was so good, there was practically no betting. Some clever people did manage to get a few sovereigns on, laying the odds of fifty to one and upwards, with foolish bookies who would take odds—on principle—about anything. I have told some time ago how Billy Marshall came to be among this few. It was the last race, and Mr. Marshall was wanting his dinner; so he decided, instead of stopping in the ring to see the race, and so being tempted to take odds, that he would lay a hundred pounds to two on Julius, and, while the race was being run, drive down to Stockbridge, get the best dinner that could be provided, and a bottle of the best to wash it down, with the two sovereigns he was going to win on the race. Daley, on Julius, looked like landing him his dinner everywhere in the race except just on the post; and here Tom French came with such a rush that the horse was done by a head, and the dinner cost poor old Billy a hundred pounds. It was an expensive feed; and, what was almost as bad, for a long time it was the cause of his having to stand a good deal of chaff.

CHAPTER XV

Some Goodwood memories—Edmund Tattersall—Shannon's
strange win—Short prices—Ben Broeck and his jockeys—A
short odds bookmaker—Sharping George Payne—Besting a
welsher

GLORIOUS GOODWOOD, what stirring reminiscences throng
the chambers of one's memory at the very mention of
it ! What troops of dead-and-gone racing men march past,
owners, trainers, jockeys, bookmakers and punters.
What giants among horses, what sensational races !
The day's hot work, with its worry and excitement, over,
what a pleasure to get down to quiet little Charlton,
Singleton, or any one of the numerous little villages
which surround the birdless groves. The pleasant
after-dinner chat in the big porch of the old cottage,
with its clinging honeysuckle and jasmine. The friendly
rubber, with a fragrant weed and glass of grog, interrupted,
now and again, by the good-tempered discussions of dear
old friends now gone for ever. How all these memories
are revived at the mention of Goodwood !

For very many years I and my set lodged at the tiny
village of Charlton, just at the western foot of the hill
as you descend from the course. One evening in the week
we were in the habit of walking through the cornfields

to the adjoining village of Singleton, where innocent frolics and sport were held, the leading spirits being Mr. Bland and Tom Trench. A good deal of money was distributed in prizes among the stable-boys and villagers on these occasions, and great fun was afforded to many ladies and gentlemen, among whom I could name some of the highest in the land. Well-known jockeys didn't think themselves above competing in foot races, jumping, and other exercises; but the pole-climbing and sack-jumping was, I believe, confined to the native rustics, and rare fun have I seen with them.

Goodwood, in the sixties, was the El Dorado of the bookmakers, and it would make the modern bookie's mouth water, as the saying goes, were I to tell some of the anecdotes I know respecting the sort of clients one had to bet with at Goodwood from forty to fifty years ago, and the sort of prices they took. There died about ten years ago a dear old client of mine, owning the most widely-known name of any on the turf, and as loved and venerated as he was widely known. I remember having to get a copy of this gentleman's bets out for the four days at Goodwood. He had had so many bets, sometimes backing five, and even more horses in a race, that he had missed some of them, and when he saw the list occupying a couple of sheets of foolscap he was perfectly appalled.

" Oh, shut it up; take it away, my lad ! " said he ; " and when old Christy settles with you, for God's sake don't show it to him. I don't want him to see what a d——d fool I've been."

Mr. Edmund Tattersall, for that was the gentleman, although he backed so many horses, rarely could be induced to have a sovereign on a favourite ; he liked to pick out three or four or more according to the size of the field, of such as he thought had chances, and back them at long prices, so I need not say he didn't often back winners ; but when he did so, it was a treat to see his handsome old face beaming with the most perfect happiness, as he went from one to another of his many friends with the news that he had backed the winner at ten to one. He was no plunger, however, his investments being usually from two to five pounds on each horse ; but even at this rate he managed to lose to me between two and three hundred pounds on the week I am speaking of ; but on that occasion I think he confined his business pretty much to myself.

I have said he would back a number of horses in the same race, and I have known times when, listening to tips, first from one authority and then another, he would back so many that he would find himself almost " round " on a race, and would come back to me with as wry a look as it was possible for such a jolly face to bear.

" Why, dash it all, Dyke," he would say, " I can't win on anything ; and if the favourite should win, I lose the lot."

I remember very well on one such occasion I remarked quite jokingly to him :

" You had better have a sovereign or two on Mr. ——'s horse ; he is very likely to win.

" Will he now ? " said he, taking me in earnest. " What's his price ? "

" One hundred to eight," was my reply.

" I'll have a hundred to eight, then," he responded.

I was amazed, because it was an unusually large amount for him to have on any one horse ; and I was very much more surprised when this horse won ; but I shall never forget the beaming radiance of his face when, after the race, he came back to thank me.

The last time I saw Mr. Tattersall I had strolled in to the sale-yard of his own famous repository, at Knightsbridge, and he was officiating in the rostrum, offering a sturdy-looking hunter. He immediately recognised me in the crowd beneath him.

" A capital horse this," he said ; and, from the corner of his eye darting a merry twinkle at me, he added : " Just the horse to carry a fourteen stone merchant to hounds." I little thought then that I should never look upon his robust old form and noble face again.

" Requiescat in pace."

One of this good client's intimate friends was very like himself in this fondness for outsiders, and he once gave me good reason for remembering it ; and, although it is so long ago, the circumstance I refer to is as fresh as possible in my memory. I was no leviathan bettor, and if I made a two hundred pounds' book on an ordinary race I thought I was doing pretty well. I had a book of that sort on the Goodwood Cup, and what a wonderful book it was! They took about evens each of two, the Derby Winner, Favonius, and the mighty Frenchman, Mortimer. Mr. Henry Saville had one in the race which was backed, on the off-chance of the two cracks cutting one another's throats—at seven or eight to one; so we were well " over round " without laying the outsider of the party, a mare called Shannon; indeed, scarcely any one backed her, and fielders considered it was so much found if, by chance, they could get a sovereign out of her at any price.

The horses were at the post and about to start, when this gentleman came up:

" What will you lay you give me a loser? " said he.

" Fifty to one," I replied, thinking I was going to find a sovereign perhaps."

" Well, I'll have 250 to 5. Which do you give me? "

" I give you Shannon, of course," I answered.

In a few minutes that extraordinary and unexplainable race was over, and the despised Shannon had won. She was my only loser, and instead of a " skinner," which most of my friends enjoyed, I lost about £40 on the race, and I never felt more wild with myself about anything because I believe I could have got the £250 back for an outlay of three sovereigns.

I very well remember once laying a young swell at Goodwood £30 to £20 a certain horse; in a minute or so he came back, having discovered he had backed the second favourite when he meant to be on the favourite.

" I find I have made a mistake, sir," he said. " Now, what will you lay me the favourite ? "

" Well, as you've made a mistake," I replied, " I will lay you thirty to twenty that one also, which is over the price."

" Put it down," he said, and walked away.

Just before the start he came running up to me with a sovereign in his hand.

" My wife has just had a tip for another in this race," said he. " What will you lay her to this sovereign, ready money ? "

This horse was a rank outsider of the party.

" Well, as it's for a lady," I replied, " I'll lay her ten to one."

" Oh, thank you so much ! " said the swell.

Now it so happened that the outsider won, and immediately after he rushed up, almost frantic with excitement and delight. I may say that all our bets, with the exception of the lady's sovereign, were settled after each race. Handing me four clean ten-pound notes, he cried exultingly :

" And now, sir, I want £10 for Mrs. Jay ! "

It is difficult for any one whose memory goes back to the Goodwood of those days to realise the fact that the very best of our native jockeys are now obliged to take a back seat among their American brethren, for, as far as I recollect, the first importation of them was anything but successful, and our Fordhams, Allcrofts, and Kitcheners found no difficulty in holding their own with the best of the Yankees.

Mr. Ten Broeck, who, by the way, commenced his racing career in England, at the Duke of Richmond's beautiful park, several years before my first appearance there, was among the very first to introduce the foreign jockey among us, and it didn't take that exceedingly cute Yankee long to find out his mistake ; and he didn't, mind you, introduce commoners of the pigskin, but the very best America could produce.

He began by running a couple in the Cup, and declaring to win with Prior, a five-year-old, with 8 stone 9 pounds, ridden by Littlefield. The other was his good mare, Prioress, which was the mount of the Yankee crack, Gilpatrick. There can be very little doubt the latter ought to have won, for she seemed fairly to run away with Gilpatrick, and had a tremendously long lead, when by some means she ran out of the course, and was not set right again until it was too late for her to have any chance, so allowing Count Lagrange's Monarque to get up and win. Still, after all, she finished among the front lot, and old Ten Broeck was so annoyed at the figure his crack jockey had cut, he settled up with him the following day, and had done with him. Some time after that, and for many years, George Fordham was his favourite jockey, and many a time in those days have I seen that great horseman carry to victory those well-known colours.

Talking of Fordham and Goodwood recalls to my memory one of the grandest races and one of the most brilliant finishes I ever remember to have seen ; and it was not for any of the great events either ; indeed, it was merely a £50 plate on the second day of the Goodwood meeting in 1864. I wonder if any of my elderly readers can call it to mind. I forget how many runners there were, but I know that the struggle between the two horses I am referring to—Crytheia and Voluptus—began in the betting ring, for both were backed, by equally determined friends, at about two to one each ; and, at the finish of the betting, it was a dead heat for favouritism, and what a struggle for mastery in the race it was ! Fordham rode Crytheia, and Morris, just then in his prime, had the mount on Voluptus. All up the straight these two, neck and neck, were at it hammer and tongs, neither being able to get the slightest advantage, and it was only just on the post that Fordham made one of those superb efforts for which he was noted, seeming to fairly lift his horse in, and secured the verdict by a nose.

I believe it was in the very next race to the one I have described that I saw Fordham on Idler and Tom Allcroft on Ascham have just such another struggle, Harry Custance being a bad third on Gownsman ; and, as in the other case, Fordham secured the verdict by a very short head.

There is a wide gulf—indeed an indescribable difference—between some of the Yankee racing men of this day, and some I knew well and did business with years ago, and somehow, I don't think the comparison favours the moderns. I may be wrong, of course, and I can only speak for myself. Take poor old Ten Broeck ; in spite of a bit of temper and a sharp tongue at times, what a gentleman he was! I remember being told that he was not very popular with his own countrymen while he was over here racing. The fact is, there were many vastly richer men than he amongst his countrymen who would have done anything to have been received by the cream of the English aristocracy—and even by royalty itself, as he was. So their dislike was probably the result of a miserable little jealousy.

I knew Mr. Ten Broeck as a rich man, respected, and indeed courted, by many of the highest in the land. When he left the scene of so many victories and of so much glory to return to his own country, I am afraid he was a poor man. I never heard the amount of his losses in the Derby of 1860, but it must have been something enormous. Mr. Merry, who was said to have netted altogether about £70,000 by the success of his horse Thormanby, won a good deal of that from Mr. Ten Broeck, who had so many cross bets with him, Umpire over Thormanby. Not satisfied with this, Mr. Ten Broeck laid against Thormanby right out, and very heavily, the same time backing his own horse Umpire to win him a tremendous stake; and Horror, which was the only horse he feared, he backed to save himself.

In the days I am dealing with, one of the best known men in the ring at Goodwood and elsewhere was Matt Collinson. It is true he did not bet anything like as heavily as Steel and Peach, or Jaques Bayliss, or like the leviathans of a later day, Richard Henry Fry, the brothers Millard, or good old Joe Pickersgill. The professional sharps he would have no dealings with, and even the regular frequenters of the ring he didn't desperately struggle after. The young beginners and the occasional comers were the sort he liked, and laid himself out to secure, and among these he had an enormous *clientèle*. It was wonderful how these people found their way to Matt; his sauve manner and the peculiar "kidment" charmed them. I have amused myself many a time watching crowds of them flocking around him with their neatly-folded fivers and tenners, eager to take of him six to four about two different horses, while an equally substantial man next door was shouting himself hoarse with ineffectual effort to lay "two to one on the field."

But while he was a favourite with the thoughtless youngsters who mostly traded with him, there were, of course, some who didn't like him.

I remember seeing him at Goodwood pay one such personage a rather large bet he had won, and as he counted out the notes to him, he thanked the gentlemen with great effusiveness, concluding with his stereotyped phrase :

"Thank you, sir, you are a gentleman."

"I wish I could say the same of you, sir," replied the young fellow, with much curtness, as he turned away.

I saw the real Matt flash up in his angry eyes, as, quick as thought, he retorted :

"You could, sir, if you'd tell as great a lie as I have."

It was at this same Goodwood meeting a young country solicitor was betting with him rather heavily, and to ready money. I heard him say :

" I tell you what it is, Mr. Collinson, if I go on like this, I shall be broken before the end of the week."

" If you are," replied Matt, " you can ask me for fifty."

" Oh, thank you, sir, you are very kind," said the solicitor, and away he went, elated to think that he had made a friend of the wealthy bookmaker.

Now it happened—perhaps naturally so—that toward the end of the meeting, on the Friday afternoon, the young man was really cleaned out. Mr. Collinson had captured all his bank ; however, he came up again smiling.

" Now, Mr. Collinson, I'm sorry I shall have to trouble you for the loan of that fifty pounds," said he ; " I want to have one more dash, and try to get some of my money back."

" I'm sorry I can't oblige you," replied Matt. " I am compelled to make a rule never to lend but one fifty pounds, and that's already out."

" What do you mean, sir ? You told me you would lend me fifty pounds if I got broken."

" No, no, sir ! there you make a mistake," answered the astute bookie. " I said, if you got broken, you might *ask* me for fifty, which, you will see, is a very different thing."

The young man didn't use many words, as he turned and walked away, but just enough to show Collinson that

o

he saw through the shabby subterfuge; but the look of contempt which he gave him, as he uttered these few words, I shall never forget, and even the thick-skinned one winced under it.

Collinson, in his early days, had his wits sharpened by much practice, for while knocking about in London, before taking to bookmaking as a profession, it was said he had to live by them, and even in prosperous days he didn't neglect his opportunities.

Goodwood was not only a little gold-mine for the bookies, it was the happy hunting-ground of the welsher and the sharper, on account of the great number of young gentlemen who were to be found making their entrance into racing life at that favourite meeting; and, of course, their inexperience made them an easy prey to these harpies, who were " got up " elaborately, and without regard to cost, for these occasions.

It was little matter of surprise that young beginners should be victimised when one knows that well-seasoned old turfites, with reputations for uncommon cuteness, did occasionally get bitten by the same people.

I remember when the late Mr. George Payne was a victim, under rather amusing circumstances. The genial old sportsman was, among other accomplishments, a first-rate story-teller, and this particular one, although it raised the laugh at his own expense, he told with great zest, and laughed at as heartily as any of his hearers. One day he was in the Victoria Station booking for Chichester among a great crowd of other swells, the day before Goodwood. There was quite a crush at the booking office, and as Mr. Payne struggled up to the window, a heavy fellow who stood head and shoulders above the others, dressed at the top of the fashion, called out, " Take a ticket for me, George ! " and, not doubting he was one of his numerous casual acquaintances, he immediately took a couple instead of one ticket, one of which he handed over the heads of the crowd to his tall friend. And then he suddenly lost him, and didn't get sight of him again till, leaning on the rails in the royal enclosure talking to old Billy Marshall on the other side, he espied him in the betting ring.

" Who is that tall gentleman, Billy ? " he inquired.

" One of the most notorious welshers in the ring, Mr. Payne," was the old bookie's reply.

I remember one occasion when a welsher had much the worst of a deal with a gentleman ; and it was a remarkable case of besting a welsher. The late lamented and beloved member for the Stroud Division of Gloucestershire, Mr. George Holloway, as everybody knows, was not much of a racing man, but he was fond of all sorts of sport, and he went to one or two of the principal races every year, rarely missing Ascot. And, mind you, he was no mere looker-on when he did go ; he had his fiver, or pony, or more down if he thought he had a good thing. He was generally accompanied by his brother Henry and the brothers Smith, from the Vale of Chalford, one a lawyer and the other a brewer, both of them very tall gentlemen, long in reach, and awkward-looking customers to tackle.

Well, it happened that while the friends were hunting about the big ring at Ascot to get the best price, " a cert." in the shape of three to one on chance, they got separated, and George found himself alone ; but hearing a substantial-looking bookie offering to take fifty to twenty, he straightway closed with the gentleman's offer, and posted his £50.

Scarcely, however, had he done so when he ran against his friends.

" What have you done ? " asked Ted Smith.

" I've laid fifty to twenty on the favourite," was the reply ; " but what have you been doing ? "

" Oh, we've been obliged to lay three to one on to that bloated, aristocratic-looking bookmaker, Walter Shakeshaft."

The Smiths, knowing a little more of racing matters than Mr. Holloway, and knowing also that a long price is not always the sign of a sound investment, felt doubtful and demanded to be made acquainted with the bookie who had taken the short odds ; and when they saw him their doubt was by no means dissipated, so it was thereupon determined to keep an eye—indeed, a number of eyes—on the said bookmaker.

" They're off ! " and the favourite got a flying start, and the nearer they got to the winning-post the more he increased his lead, which fact Mr. Holloway's bookie was aware of, and the circumstance had an evidently disturbing influence upon him, for he and his clerk were making tracks for the exit gate. Suddenly he feels a grip as of iron on his collar, and he is confronted with Mr. Holloway and the two awkward-looking brothers.

"Oh, I'll give you your money back!" groaned the craven scoundrel, fearful lest other of his clients should see how matters stood.

"My friend wants £70, and not a penny less," said Mr. Smith; and the £70 were immediately forthcoming, and the welsher bolted.

While all this was taking place, the race was being finished, and it appeared that when the favourite came to tackle the stiff bit of finish he stopped to nothing, and something got up and beat him by a head.

"Oh, dear me!" said Mr. Holloway, "why, I've lost the money after all." And he seemed positively distressed because he couldn't find the welsher to return him —at least—his own £20.

CHAPTER XVI

Gamblers and gambling—Hazards—Jem Mace—Charley Chappell—and the parson—Inveterate gamblers—Frank Leleu finds a playfellow—Charles Head's lucky start

FORTY years ago, and previous to that, no first-class race-meeting was complete without its company of travelling gamblers, with green baize-covered tables, roulette machinery, and dice for hazard. They usually rented luxuriously furnished rooms in a private house, for which, I suppose, they would have to pay a pretty high figure. Spirits, champagnes of crack brands, and other expensive wines, with high-class cigars, were supplied gratuitously, and *ad libitum*, to the young swells who nightly thronged these rooms. They were not always confined to private houses, for at some places—as at Doncaster, for instance —they made arrangements with the owners of the public subscription rooms, and play was permitted in well-arranged chambers on these premises.

That the heavy and at times ruinous play could have been carried on in this semi-public manner without the slightest interference on the part of the authorities proves how great is the change which has come over us since those days. What would the Anti-Gambling League say to this state of things?

It must not be supposed that because the managers of those rooms were so lavish in their expenditure upon their clients they were a set of swindlers, playing with loaded dice. I should be sorry to infer anything of the kind. I believe the rooms I am now referring to were conducted fairly as far as the play went, for on many occasions I have known the half-drunken and perfectly reckless young fools play so heavily and so luckily that the owners of the tables, or bankers as they were called, have declared the bank broken, and the play over for the night; which would never be the case if they were playing with loaded dice. The turnover at these establishments was so enormous that the slight advantage of about twenty-one to twenty—which it is admitted they had in honest play—was quite sufficient to account for their lavish expenditure, and also for the large fortunes which have, in some cases, been made at the game.

While I assert that the first-class rooms were conducted fairly, I am bound to admit there were to be found at the same time travellers, in like way of business, most unscrupulous rogues, who would stand at nothing when they got a flat in their net. I was once, in my salad days, one of these flats, and found myself in one of their traps. On my very first visit to Newmarket I was politely invited, after the first day's racing, to spend a few hours in the evening at the lodgings of a fellow-townsman about whom I knew nothing, but who would, I was made to understand, afford us an opportunity for a little innocent game. The game was chicken hazard, which was new to me, and, naturally enough, I had to pay for my experience. I knew afterwards that, in this case, I was taking on a man with whom I had not a thousand to one chance.

It is unnecessary I should give the name. He afterwards became a well-known bookmaker, and an owner of race-horses in training at Newmarket.

In subsequent visits to Newmarket I became acquainted with the travelling gamblers of the better sort, and had opportunities of seeing roulette and hazard played under other conditions, and have witnessed thousands—hundreds of thousands ; yea, perhaps millions—of pounds change hands, where old Joe Wood bossed the show and the eagle-eyed " Arthur " wielded the croupier's rake. I remember one night at Newmarket, while sitting under the presidency of this able old croupier, the renowned Jem Mace came into the room, accompanied by Sam Haley, a brother bruiser, with whom he had, during that day, made his first attempt at bookmaking.

They were then in the heyday of their glory, both having recently won important battles. Mace lodged with our party at a private house near the station ; and I have reason to know they had a good *bank* with which to make a beginning as bookmakers ; but the truth is they would have needed no bank at all if they had had the least knowledge of the business : the young students from Cambridge and many other young swells vied with each other for the honour of betting with these celebrities, eagerly doing business on any terms. The new fielders, however, were not clever enough to take advantage of this splendid opportunity, or they would have made a fortune rapidly. As it was their day's work showed a very considerable addition to the bank.

Well, it was rather late the same night when they saw, for the first time, Mr. Wood's elegant apartments. Flushed with the success which had attended their first day's bookmaking they took seats at the green baize-covered table very near to myself. They were interested spectators of the game for a short time only. Then they began to nibble at it themselves, in a small way; and, losing, they were very soon playing for higher stakes; and, again losing, playing for still higher stakes. In an hour they lost a large part of the day's profits. It now looked so like the game breaking them I ventured to suggest they would be wise to go home with me—all in vain. They were bound as firmly to their seats as had they tenpenny nails through their legs. They were so deep in the hole they would go deeper still, or get their money back. The result was that when obliged to go home they were thoroughly cleaned out, and the next morning found them pawning their jewellery to provide another bank.

Of course, one occasionally witnessed strange scenes at these gaming-rooms, but I never saw the slightest approach to rowdyism; and any attempts at " besting " a youngster on the part of the old sharp were promptly stopped by Arthur.

There are probably still living a few sporting swells who will remember the rosy-faced, good-looking and stylishly got up Charley Chappell. Many of them would perhaps like to forget him ; the very mention of him will revive unpleasant recollections. Fifty years ago and more Chappell's was a well-known figure in racing circles ; he attended all the principal race-meetings throughout the country, having well-appointed rooms wherever he went, which were the resort of fast young swells and hardened old gamblers alike. For these people the excitement and betting which the day's racing afforded were not sufficient. So, after a good dinner, probably with a copious supply of champagne, they felt themselves just fit to tackle Mr. Chappell and his clever assistants at the roulette or hazard tables ; and the rosy one was always ready to oblige them, not only providing the necessary tools for these games, but as much more champagne, soda and brandy or other drink as they could manage to consume. And there is no doubt that very often old Charley netted some fine fish. Still I have often heard him swear that he was a mere jackal for the bookmakers. He provided, during his intercourse with the aforesaid swells, any quantity—and the very best—of the good things of this life, and straightway delivered them up to the " bloated fielders." Poor old Charley was indeed an inveterate punter, and although he is reported to have made fabulous sums at his own game, I am afraid he was in but poorish circumstances when he died, some twenty-six years ago.

Excepting good old George Hodgman I suppose there is not a racing man living to-day who will remember Chappell's master and predecessor in the same line—Durden. He died while the writer was a promising youth, groaning through the dreary years of apprenticeship. Hence I am unable to speak of him from personal acquaintance, and therefore not with that freedom which springs from a consciousness that I am conveying to my readers the truth. I was once privileged to spend an evening with one of the oldest and most respected betting men in England, who retired on a large fortune, before some of the present race of bookies were born ; to this gentleman I am indebted for what I know of Durden, and one or two stories he told me are so good I will venture to repeat them here.

Outside his profession Durden was one of the greatest sharps that ever lived, and at the same time a most perfect " take-down," because he didn't look it. On the contrary, he had a sober, old-fashioned look about him which disarmed suspicion, and almost a clerical appearance which marvellously assisted him in his wily purposes. Many are the stories which are told of him—all of them desperately wicked—but some redeemed by the fact that they afforded amusement to hundreds of his contemporaries, and now I hope they may do the like for many thousands belonging to a generation which knew him not.

On one occasion when he was working the tables at Abergavenny Races, he was pestered by a young fool who, having lost some money to him at roulette, thought himself entitled to hang on to him wherever he went. They were staying at an old-fashioned hotel. Durden had found his way into the spacious kitchen, where, as he bargained for, the youngster followed him. The ceiling was well hung with flitches of home-cured bacon and prime hams which the young man began to admire.

" Why don't you ask the landlord to give you one of the hams ? " asked Durden.

" I'm not fool enough to do that," replied his companion, " and he'd not be fool enough to give me one if I did."

" Oh yes he would," replied the crafty old man. " You have no idea how generous these Welsh folks are ; they're as generous as they are honest."

Now the young man, while he thought they might be the most honest people in the world, had not been impressed in any very remarkable manner with the fact ; and with regard to their generosity, the treatment he had received at the hands of this very landlord had assured him that if it was a national characteristic, the landlord didn't possess it, so he concluded it would be a pretty safe thing to bet about.

" Well, will you back your opinion, Durden ? " he asked.

" Yes, I will, for whatever you like," answered the old man.

" Then I'll bet you a pony he won't make me a present of one of those fine hams for merely asking."

" Done ! " said Durden ; " that's a bet."

The dupe wouldn't allow the old man to leave the kitchen, but insisted that he should go alone to the landlord who was in the bar-parlour, and put the question in his own way. This was agreed to, and the young man proceeded to test the question. Walking into the parlour in an unconcerned manner, he addressed the landlord:

" Nice lot of hams, Mr. Owen, in the kitchen ; shouldn't mind begging one of them, if you are in a giving humour ! "

" I'll give *you* one with pleasure, sir," replied the host, " and you'll find it as good as it looks."

Of course Old Durden had readied the landlord, so that prime ham cost the young fool about eighteen shillings a pound.

Durden was fond of laying traps for unwary friends to fall into. He was walking one afternoon in Hyde Park, and, as was most likely to happen, he chanced to run against one of his numerous playfellows—a young aristocrat. While they stopped to speak a groom came prancing along on a magnificent hack.

" Look at that lovely chestnut ! " exclaims the swell.

" He is a beauty," replied Durden, " but not a chestnut. He's a bay."

" Bay be d——d ! " replied the swell. " You've been looking so long on green baize you've gone colour blind. It's a bright chestnut, I tell you."

" No, no, my lord ; it's distinctly a bay," replied the wily old man.

" A chestnut for a hundred," said the swell.

Durden protested he didn't want to bet ; he wouldn't like to rob his lordship ; but rather sneeringly concluded by hinting that the swell knew nothing of horses or their colour.

" Damn it, bet me a hundred, then ! " cried the exasperated nobleman.

" Done then, just to oblige your lordship," replied Durden.

" But who shall decide the bet ? "

" Oh, we'll leave it to the groom who is riding him," answered the victim. " See, he is coming by again."

This was settled, and the groom was stopped. His lordship said :

" That's a charming hack, my man, but what do you call his colour ? "

" He's a bright bay, sir," the groom replied.

The swindled nobleman looked for a moment as the beautiful creature began to caracole and caper about, then dashed down the Row at a great pace.

" Well, that beats cock-fighting," he said. " I think the Park's full of colour-blind folks or infernal idiots this afternoon ! "

He agreed however that he had fairly lost the hundred pounds ; nevertheless, he hung about the Park for a long time in the hope of seeing the groom and his beautiful horse come by again. Of course, having already done a good day's work, he didn't come that way again ; and I suppose I needn't tell my readers that Mr. Durden was not wholly unacquainted with that groom.

Durden once found himself *tête-à-tête* in a railway carriage with a simple looking old clergyman bound for a long journey to the same town. Durden began talking about horses and racing and betting, and, as was natural, it was soon clear they held extremely opposite views on these subjects and each expressed his own with some warmth.

" I think betting in all forms a crime, and the greatest curse on the earth, and under no circumstances would I be guilty of it," said the parson.

" Now that's very unfortunate," answered Durden, " for I was going to do you a good turn. I wanted you to have a sovereign on a horse of mine at the races to-morrow. It will only be an even money chance, but it's sure to win."

" Oh dear no ! Not a shilling, were it ever such a good thing ! " answered the parson.

" Well, but this is an absolute certainty," urged Mr. Durden. " No risk whatever, so there really is no gambling about it. Indeed so sure is it to win I wouldn't mind paying you the sovereign to-day which you would be certain to win if you invested it on the race to-morrow."

He made this tempting offer, being curious to know how far the parson's objection to betting was founded on principle, and he was not greatly surprised when he found the good man after very little persuasion willing to bet on these terms. So the bet was made and the sovereign duly paid over to the parson, whereupon he was favourably impressed with his fellow-traveller's liberality and he began to think he had been over-harsh in his judgment of these betting men.

Durden, seeing how the land lay, thought it was now time to try to recover his sovereign with a little interest, so he introduced a couple of beautiful scarf-pins carefully wrapped in cotton wool. They appeared to be of bright gold with a small diamond in an enamelled setting.

He pitched a plausible story of getting them at half their value of a friend in the trade who was about to become bankrupt. One he wanted as a present to his nephew, the other he wouldn't mind parting with for what it had cost him, £2 5s. There was no doubt the shopkeeper's price would be three times that amount.

As he had expected, the parson, now full of faith in his generous friend, and full also of that weakness for a good bargain inherent in human nature and from which parsons even are not exempt, eagerly bit, a deal being effected on these terms. Need I say that the diamond was a bit of good French paste mounted in real Brummagem gold, worth probably five shillings? Durden often boasted of this swindle, which was perpetrated not for the sake of the sovereign profit, but for the fun of the thing; and to punish the parson for his greed and hypocrisy, knowing also that he could practise on him with impunity, after the betting experience.

Most of my sporting readers will remember Frank Leleu, a fish merchant in a very large way of business in London, who attended the better sort of race-meetings throughout the year, and who was known at one time as one of our heaviest punters. Frank didn't confine himself by any means to betting on horses; he was at heart such a dear lover of a gamble he would bet on anything. He indulged this propensity at cards; and at his favourite club he would bet very heavily at billiards also ; and there was a time when the baize-covered table and the merry rattle of the little box had a wonderful charm for him. The story I am about to relate is perfectly true, and demonstrates in a marvellous manner how strong in him was this passion for gambling.

As I have said, about forty years ago Stockbridge was one of the best attended and most fashionable meetings in the country, and one Leleu never missed. On the occasion to which I allude, he had had a day's racing at Odiham, and at its conclusion he made tracks for the quiet little village of Wallop, which is not very far from the Stockbridge course, and where he was to stay for the races. To his immense annoyance, he found on his arrival that he was the only person staying at the inn. So after a solitary and miserable dinner he sallied out in the hope of finding company ; for him to get through a night without play of some sort seemed an impossibility, if not an uncanny thing ; and he was certain he wouldn't rest if he attempted it. He found the village in the same condition as his hotel. At present none of the visitors had arrived. It was a wretched, drizzling sort of night when he made his way back to the inn after his unsuccessful prowl, and he was about turning in when he caught sight of the only human being he had been able to recognise as a sport of any kind.

This was a slim young fellow, evidently poor but not disreputable in appearance, and whom he at once remembered as a sort of runner for the bookies, who varied this

P

employment by occasionally adopting the rôle of tipster, if not sometimes an even still humbler occupation.

"Hi! ho! What are you doing here, shaver?" asked Frank.

"I've come on from Odiham, Mr. Leleu," said the young man, "to be ready for Stockbridge to-morrow."

Then Leleu invited the sharp young fellow to have a drink, for which he found the young man not at all indisposed. After the dose had been repeated Mr. Leleu opened up the matter next to his heart.

"Look here, young fellow," said he, "did you ever play hazard?"

"Yes, sir, a very little," he replied.

"Well, as there is nothing going on here to-night we'll play," said Frank, producing the tools.

"Oh, no, I can't play, Mr. Leleu! I've got no money to play with," was the answer to this challenge.

"Well, look here, I'll lend you a fiver to start with," replied Frank, and finding the young fellow not slow to accept such an offer, he did actually lend him five pounds, with which he allowed this needy person to play against all he carried about him; and he did this not, as some hasty readers may conclude, because he was a fool—those who knew Mr. Leleu would never accuse him of being that—but simply because his passion for play was so strong, he would rather play with no possibility of winning than not play at all, and a fiver was of small moment to him; but, fortunately for the young man, in trying to recapture the fiver, Leleu lost a good many fivers ; indeed, at the end of the night's diversion one of the players was a richer man than he had ever been before, walking away from the inn with nearly a hundred pounds, after having repaid the fiver. He won also a pressing invitation to return the following night to give Mr. Leleu his revenge : this invitation, likewise, he availed himself of, and with such result that, in a pecuniary sense, he never " looked back " after it. He had converted his borrowed fiver into seven or eight hundred pounds, which he immediately invested in what was, in those days, the extremely lucrative business of bookmaking.

This poor young fellow was endowed with abilities of a very high order He had great aptitude for figures, a cool, well-stocked head, immense energy, and a ready and brilliant wit, never equalled or approached among bookmakers of my time. These qualities soon won for him a foremost place in the profession ; and in a few years he was a man of large means. He had theatres and music-halls in London ; some useful horses on the turf, and one of the very largest and most profitable connections among bookmakers. To old racing men I am sure I need not announce that the great bookmaker to whom Frank Leleu had afforded this singular start in life was none other than the celebrated Charles Head.

There are few games which obtain and exercise such complete mastery over the human will as hazard, and it is really very difficult to understand why this should be so. It calls forth none of the higher qualities of the mind as does chess, cribbage, and whist, and it demands no great power of nerve and skill of hand as at billiards. Yet the rattle of the magic box is sweeter in the ears of its votaries than all Cecilia's charms, and more potent to fascinate poor mortals than any siren who ever bewitched them to destruction.

Bill—or perhaps I had better call him by the name he was best known by, Farmer Quartley—was one of the strange characters whom I have met with on the turf. There was scarcely a game of any kind or a form of gambling with which Mr. Quartley was not acquainted; indeed, I may say, at which he was not an adept; but of all games, I think hazard was his favourite. He had gone down West for races, held near the delightful old city of Exeter, his headquarters being the New London Hotel, where was staying also a fair-faced betting man hailing from another West-country cathedral city, but nearer the Midlands, and whom, for this purpose, I will call Mr. Henry. This young man, like Quartley, had a passion for the box and dice, and coming into the hotel about eleven o'clock, the first night, with the intention of having a turn at hazards with the old man, he was surprised to find he had retired for the night at that unheard of early hour. The fact was, Quartley was really very unwell.

Henry marched up to the old man's room; and quietly knocked. There was no reply; he knocked a little louder; still no reply. Then taking the little box out of his pocket, he slipped the bits of ivory in, giving it the magic rattle; and in a moment Quartley jumped out of bed, the door was flung open, and in another minute, ill as he was, he was calling the main.

After playing for a couple of hours and winning a considerable amount, the old man declared he would not play any longer. This didn't suit Mr. Henry ; and after a good deal of wrangling, Quartley bluntly ordered him to leave the room. Henry walked to the door and quietly locked it, and opening the window, threw the key into the yard below.

" You understand that, Master Farmer, I suppose ? " said he. " I came here to make a night of it, and I don't intend you to sneak off to bed now you've won a few pounds."

So the farmer was almost compelled to play on, much against his wish, as he was really ill ; but a friend of Henry's tells me that it would have been much better for that young gentleman had he retired earlier, instead of throwing away the key.

As the author of some funny stories, and chief actor in most of them, I propose devoting a chapter wholly to this remarkable turfite, Mr. William Quartley.

CHAPTER XVII

Gamblers and gambling — "Farmer" Quartley — Hazards at
sea—Diamond cut diamond—Lord Marcus Beresford's slight
mistake

IN a somewhat chequered journey through life, I have
been a keen observer of the many specimens of my fellow-
travellers, and I can honestly say I have made earnest
effort to see all sides of them, and can also truthfully say
that while I have not been fortunate enough to make the
acquaintance of many quite perfect men and women—such
as are plentiful in the writings of certain novelists—I have
rarely met with humanity so utterly degraded and worthless as not to disclose, on acquaintance, some redeeming
qualities. Of course, one would not seek among the
habitués of the turf for what are known in this world as
saints; but I am thankful to say it is not a history of
saints I am writing, nor even a history of perfect men and
women. I haven't at hand the material for such a work;
my characters are all sketches from real life, and do
mostly relate to men who were very human; which will
account for their being, more or less, sinners.

Everybody knows that too much of the residue of the
rascality of this great and pious country finds its way
on to what is known as " the turf "; but what racing men

properly object to is that ignorant and unthinking goody-goody folk should persist in looking on this sediment, and speaking of it, as " the turf."

Would it be fair, because the pious Jabez Balfour & Co. were a set of unmitigated scoundrels, to look upon the general body of chapel-goers and professors of religion as a huge mass of canting hypocrisy, intent only on schemes for the plunder of trustful widows and helpless orphans ? No, no, my friends, the congregations of betting men are much like your own congregations, composed of all sorts, good and bad. I have in my time seen something of both ; have found, I am bound to say, among religionists some of the gentlest and noblest human beings I have known in all my journey ; but believe me, when I declare, that in matters of integrity, honour, and goodness of heart, the respectable members of the betting ring are comparable with any profession or class in the country.

In these reminiscences of the turf it is my purpose to make my readers acquainted with the good and bad, and also with some very much mixed specimens of racing people.

In the course of an acquaintance extending over at least a quarter of a century, I saw a good deal of Mr. Quartley—had, indeed, very many transactions with him —and had ample opportunity of observing his varied characteristics, which I may say I did not neglect.

He was well known to most London sportsmen, because his home was there for many years. His burly figure was a familiar one on race-courses and in betting rings all over England; but as he originally hailed from the West, it was at the little West-country meetings he was best known. The farmer was in many respects a remarkable man. He hadn't been blessed in early life with a university education; indeed, in the matter of booklearning I am afraid he had been sadly neglected. To use a word he was very fond of using, he was no " grammarmatician." For all that, he had a ready wit and strong common-sense, and these enabled him to take his own part in such company as he was in the habit of consorting with. It is true he knew but one language, but that he spoke with such forcibleness, that in a war of words he was seldom defeated; but of all his accomplishments that which he prided himself most about was his knowledge of all gambling games. He was, all through his life, an inveterate gamester; and as he was not in the habit of over-handicapping himself, or taking on very difficult jobs, he was, as a rule, able to hold his own—and generally a little of his opponent's—at any game.

He was a tricky billiard player, but—like a certain eminent fielder who was fond of billiards, and played fairly well—he wasn't an elegant player; indeed, from the way he held his cue and jerked himself about, innocent strangers picked him up for a jay at the game, and only dropped him when their money was gone, and they had arrived at a different conclusion.

As I have already intimated, one of the farmer's favourite games was hazard, at which he was an adept, and many are the startling feats he is said to have accomplished with the bits of ivory.

I once heard him declare that if he had never dabbled with keeping and backing horses, but had taken care of all the money he had won at hazards, he would have been a rich man. Sometimes he played with people who didn't take their losses kindly ; some getting a notion into their heads that the dice were loaded, or some other unfair means employed. On one occasion something of the kind happened under circumstances which upset the farmer's usually strong nerves. He was attending Weymouth Races in company with two West-country betting men, one of them at the present time alive, and both at one time extensive S.P. merchants. They put up at the Victoria Hotel and there fell in with the owner of a yacht, which lay out in the bay. Rather late in the evening they began playing hazard, and after watching it for some time the gentleman began to nibble ; and at eleven o'clock, having lost a few pounds, he was pinned down to the table with the hot determination to get it back. It was after Mr. Bruce's Act became law, so eleven o'clock was closing time, and the host could not be prevailed upon to allow the game to continue, or the gentleman whose bed was aboard the yacht to remain any longer in the house.

" Look here, my lads," says he, " my man is opposite the door here with the dinghy, waiting for me ; come aboard my yacht for an hour and finish the play. I've plenty of good stuff to drink there, and some good cigars."

The two younger men were for accepting at once this

pressing invitation ; the more cautious old farmer didn't like trusting himself on an element where he didn't feel at home ; but after a while he yielded, and all four went over to the dinghy ; and very soon they were cutting through the sea in dreadful darkness, and Quartley felt very uncomfortable until he was safely aboard the yacht, and even then he was not particularly easy in his mind.

Play commenced with the accompaniment of good cigars and drinks, and they were all very jolly till about two o'clock in the morning, when the farmer declared they had played and drunk enough, and he would be going back to shore. The yachtsman's bad luck had followed him aboard, and he had by this time lost a considerable sum. He was a powerful man, and under the influence of the drink looked fierce, and capable of executing any threat he might make.

" I'll tell you what it is, gentlemen," said he. " I'll blow out the bottom of the damned dinghy rather than she shall take you back before I have had another hour's play." So he compelled them to go on with the game, and as his bad luck continued, or his bad play, or for some other reason, he kept on losing ; at the end of the hour he had lost all the money the yacht contained, and was a considerable sum in debt.

The farmer, happening to raise his eyes, saw what made him very uneasy ; this was another pair of eyes looking straight into his, bright and keen as his own. Looking from the strange eyes to the owner of them, he saw a strongly-built, middle-aged sailor fellow, with a sinister look about him, threatening trouble.

" Don't be alarmed, stranger," said the sailor, when he found he was discovered, " I've been here a-watching of you gents a good time."

" And what the devil business had you doing anything of the kind ? " asked the gentleman. " It's no part of my steward's business to be watching me or my friends. What do you mean, sir ? "

" You know me, master," replied the man ; " and you ought to know I wouldn't do sich wi'out good reason. Come into my cabin, sir, and I'll tell what'll surprise you ! "

The gentleman rose to follow his steward, and while addressing himself to his servant, fixed his eyes on his guests.

" No foul play, I hope, Jack ? By God, if there is I'll scuttle the damned ship but I'll pay somebody for it ! "

The condition of the farmer and his friends may be imagined while the couple were shut up in the adjoining cabin. Either of them would have given their winnings two or three times told to have been safely bedded down in the Victoria Hotel at that moment. They were perfectly aware how much they should be overmatched by the yachtsman and his hands if it came to strife. Still, the old man, in the frightful anxiety and suspense of the time, never lost his wits. It was lucky for them all he didn't. The first thing he did was to wrap some little matters in paper, and then throw the parcel through the open cabin window into the sea. He could hear the loud and angry voice of the yachtsman in the steward's cabin, but he couldn't make out what was said. When at last the door was opened, he heard the master roar out :

" Shake up every man aboard, Jack, and bring them into my cabin ! "

This order boded no good to Quartley and his friends ; but whatever they may have felt, when the gentleman re-entered the cabin they put on a bold front, and the farmer, knowing how useful it is to get in the first good knock, started at once with well-affected indignation.

" What does this treatment mean, sir ? " he inquired. " I thought we were playing with a gentleman."

" You'll soon discover, sir, that you have been playing with a gentleman," answered the yachtsman, emphasising the word " playing " ; " and a funny devil you'll find you've been playing with, before I have done with you, if you can't disprove what my steward charges against you."

" Charges against me, sir ? " said the old man, in a voice almost choked between simulated rage and injured innocence.

" Yes, against you, sir ! " cried Jack, coming forward at the moment with four strapping young fellows at his heels. " I say you have been cheating the master, for I saw you change the dice several times."

" Oh, you—you wicked wretch ! " cried Quartley, apparently appalled with the enormity of the fellow's wickedness. " May I go to the bottom of the sea before I reach the shore if I've more than the one set of honest dice about me ! "

" If you have not, perhaps one of your friends has," said the gentleman, a little cooler, and evidently somewhat shaken by the tone and attitude of injured virtue, so well acted by the farmer.

" Well, if you are all so innocent, you and your friends won't object to be searched," put in the steward.

" Searched ! " almost screamed the farmer. " Who are you to talk of searching gentlemen ? "

" Well, if you are innocent, you wouldn't object to being searched," said the yachtsman ; " and all I can say is, that you'll be searched either with your consent or without it, and if loaded dice are not found upon you, you shall be taken ashore at once ; but if they are, why, as I'm captain of this ship, you shall all three have something to remember her by as long as you live."

" I would fight till I died," replied the old man, " before I would submit to such a thing at the dictation of a man like that," dramatically pointing to the steward ; " but if you desire such a thing I am perfectly willing to submit, and if you find on me or on either of my friends anything which warrants this brutal conduct, do what you like with us."

This ingenuous and well-acted little speech took the wind out of the enemies' sails, but it didn't prevent the search ; and what a search it was ! The three friends were required to strip to the skin. This indignity they stoutly protested against, and only submitted to when they saw preparations for using force.

It was very comical to see the three friends standing there, each guarded by a couple of stalwart fellows, and wrapped in blankets, while the whole of their clothing was being carefully examined. My readers are, of course, prepared for the result of the search—nothing to incriminate them was found; so their clothing being restored to its proper uses, the farmer, again assuming the air of injured innocence, said :

"Now, sir, I hope you are satisfied you have been playing with gentlemen ? "

"Well, I can't say I am satisfied, sir," replied the yachtsman, " but I've given you my word, and you may go. My man still swears he saw foul play, and I believe him, but in some way you have been too many for me. Get off, and thank your lucky stars."

The dinghy was brought round by a couple of the sailors and the three friends stowed in her. A fresh breeze had sprung up while they had been in the yacht ; above their heads was a darkness dreadful in its density and beneath them the now turbulent sea yawned black and awful. Beyond all reality the situation seemed terrible to their excited minds ; the voice of the malicious steward coming out of the darkness increased their fear.

" You know what to do with the scamps, my lads," said the voice with sinister suggestiveness.

Of course the farmer and his pals put the most awful construction on the steward's words, but fear didn't quite depose the old man's reason nor rob him of all his natural cunning.

"Look here, my men," said he, addressing himself to the sailors, "it's a nasty, dangerous job to be fetched out of your warm bunks for, but you land us safely on yonder beach and there's a fiver a-piece for you."

"All right, gentlemen, we'll put you ashore in a jiffey," answered one of the men.

In ten minutes more the sailors had earned and received their money, and Quartley never in his life disbursed a tenner with more pleasure.

"Never no more, my boys, never no more will you find William Quartley taking on this sort of job on the briny," said he.

During one Goodwood Meeting many years ago, Quartley made one of a party of five who had taken a cottage at the pretty village of Singleton for the week, and among the party was a man in many respects very like the farmer. He was a wideawake fellow, cute and clever, but very unscrupulous, and was frequently taking down even his own pals with "put-up" jobs. He was a tall, thin, one-eyed man, with a rather eccentric get-up—parsonic suit of black, with a white top hat, very low in the crown and broad in the brim, which he must have had specially made, for no one ever saw such a head-gear the like of it, and he was known among his friends as Bos. The little incident I am about to relate concerning this man and the farmer shows how very possible it is for the sharpest biter to be bitten; is, indeed, a neat case of diamond cut diamond.

The first morning after the party's arrival at Singleton the farmer awoke about six o'clock, and turned out with the intention of walking up to the course before breakfast, a distance of about three miles. He knew the walk would prepare him for the substantial meal provided, and he thought it possible that among the horses and jockeys who would be doing their morning's work there, he might pick up something which would be useful later in the day; but he was fortunate enough to fall across this something useful long before he reached the course. It is a stiffish hill for a fat man with a corporation and habits such as our farmer's; so when about half-way up he sat on a stile and dropped into profound thought. I don't suppose the marvellous landscape, stretching out before his eyes like a beautiful panorama, of wooded hills and fertile vales, bathed in all the golden glory of the early morn, charmed him as did the sight of a huge flock of sheep browsing on the slopes of that hill, for in this flock of sheep he saw what was more to him than gorgeous scenery—a possibility of making a bit.

As he sat turning this possibility over in his mind, he saw the owner of the sheep, a rosy-faced, good-tempered farmer, come striding across the field toward him.

"Good morning, farmer!" said Quartley. "These be a nice lot of sheep you have here; they be yours, I guess?"

"Yes, they are mine, and they are a flock of nice sheep," replied the farmer.

"Can you tell me the exact number in this flock, farmer?" asked Quartley.

"Yes; there are three hundred and seventy-five in this flock; but it's a very funny thing, I was asked the same question half an hour ago by a gentleman who sat on that very seat. And he was very particular to have the exact number."

"Indeed! that is remarkable; but what sort of a man was he, sir?"

"Well, he was a sort of man once seen never forgotten; he was a one-eyed chap dressed in a suit of black, a bit like a parson, but with a funny white hat on."

As the farmer made this reply Quartley's eyes fairly scintillated with the fun of the situation and the possibilities hidden behind it.

"Now look here, farmer," he said, "I know that young gentleman and I know what his little game is; and what's more, I mean to spoil it, and I want you to help me."

And then he painted his friend Bos in such colours as easily induced the simple countryman to lend himself to Quartley's wily purposes. Instead of finishing his journey up the hill he descended to the village, not wishing, at present, to run against Bos, who he now knew had gone up to the course before him.

A couple of hours before the time of the first race the party of five was in the wagonette which had been

Q

ordered, and the poor horse was struggling up the hill toward the course. When they reached the stile Bos ordered the driver to pull up and give the poor animal a rest.

" Fine flock of sheep," naturally enough remarked one of the party.

" It is a nice flock," said Bos. " I wonder how many there are in it ? "

And then some of them began guessing, but Quartley appeared but little interested in the discussion ; but when Bos proposed they should each one have a guess for a sweepstake of a sovereign each he readily joined them in it. Each one wrote the number he guessed against his own initials on a sheet of paper. Some of the party were very wide of the mark. Quartley and his friend Bos were as my readers feel assured much nearer. Bos guessed 370, Quartley 360.

" Me over anybody for a fiver," said Bos.

" Done ! " replied Quartley, " make it a tenner."

This of course Bos was only too delighted to accommodate him with ; and so hot did both get over the matter that the betting only ended when Quartley had staked his last sovereign in the hands of one of the gentlemen who were present, for he had wisely insisted on having no credit in a bet of this kind. And so the stakeholder held £80 between them.

" How shall the bet be decided ? " asked Quartley, " it will be a big job to count them."

" Perhaps this is the farmer coming across the field,"

said Bos, " if it is we will let him decide it. But let no one be allowed to speak to him but Mr. Smith."

This reasonable condition being assented to by both sides, Mr. Smith addressed the gentleman as he approached, " Will you be good enough to tell us if this is your flock of sheep, sir ? "

" Yes, it is, sir," answered the farmer.

" If you know the exact number will you be kind enough to tell us that also, just to decide a little wager ? " said Smith.

" Certainly, with pleasure ! There's exactly 350 sheep in that flock," replied the farmer.

" Three hundred and fifty ! " almost screamed Bos. " Are you sure you haven't made a mistake, farmer ? "

" No, I've made no mistake, sir," replied the farmer, " there were 375 when you asked me at six o'clock this morning, but I've drawn out twenty-five of the fattest for the market."

And the company, finding how the crafty Bos had fallen into his own trap, didn't spare him, nor was he for a long time allowed to forget the circumstance.

CHAPTER XVIII

Cases of mistaken identity—Sir John Astley's claim—Lord Marcus Beresford—A fistic preacher—Taking a liberty

SIR JOHN ASTLEY was a frequent client of mine, and a more agreeable man to do business with one could not desire. An English gentleman in the true sense of the word was the bluff and jolly Sir John. There were no airs of the superior creature about him such as belonged to many of the swells I knew so well, and whom in too many cases I have powerful reasons to remember—the sort of people who condescended to do business with you, making you feel the while that you must belong to another order of humanity, and that they only submit to the contract because it suits their purpose, and often, I verily believe, they consider themselves conferring an honour upon you by getting into your debt and remaining there.

Sir John was not only the most genial of sportsmen, he was the soul of honour, and I am sure he would have been the last man in the world to make an unjust claim. Yet he was mortal and therefore fallible ; and on one occasion he made a claim upon me for £500 which I did not owe. The claim was made on behalf of Sir John by the gentleman who did his settling for many years, Mr. Henry Emmerson, otherwise known as " Black Harry." Now Master Harry, although, I believe, as straight as a gun-barrel, and a good sort of fellow at bottom, was by no means a meek-and-mild sort of person, and was apt occasionally to use English of an extremely forcible and not altogether classical description. He knocked me almost senseless and entirely upset my equilibrium one Monday at the Victoria Club by demanding in his usual stentorian voice and peremptory manner the trifle of £500 for Sir John Astley.

" I don't owe Sir John £500, or any other sum," I replied.

" Don't you," retorted my *fair* friend ; " he says you do, so make haste and pull it out."

" But what is it for ? " I asked. " I have had no bet with Sir John, I assure you."

" I don't know nor care what it's for ; he's got you down for £500 and you'll have to part."

" I don't owe it," I repeated passionately, " and what is more, whatever the consequences I will never pay it."

After more hot words on both sides it was decided to defer the dispute until we reached Tattersall's in the afternoon ; and in the meantime he would send to Sir John for particulars of the bet. I had been for months past having a very bad time, and the last week had added considerably to my misfortunes ; and now, on the top of it all to have an unjust claim made upon me for what was at the time a very large amount, filled me

with dismay, and I am sure could even Emmerson have
known my feelings at the moment he would have exercised
a little more gentleness. At Tattersall's the argument
was reopened. Unquestionably Sir John had got the bet
down in his book to me clear enough, and just as clearly
my book showed no transaction ; and as I had but a very
small book on that particular race, one certainly of not
more than £100, I could not possibly have laid £500
against any horse. I was aware this argument would
avail me little if Sir John still believed I was the man
he had betted with. I promised to see him the following day, my only hope now being that I might be able
to convince him that the mistake was his, and if I really
could not convince him I made up my mind that I would
under no circumstances pay it, so strongly did I feel the
injustice of it, although I was aware that the consequences
would be in all probability a " warning-off " order
against me.

The next day I saw Sir John, produced my book and
tried to impress him with the improbability of my laying
such a bet under the circumstances, using the strongest
language I could command, for apart from the seriousness
of the matter to myself, I felt really anxious not to quarrel
with one whom I so entirely respected, and who, I knew,
had simply mistaken me for another. I felt he was incapable of saying the thing he did not believe ; but, alas !
all my eloquence was wasted upon him.

" Damn it all, Dyke ! " he said, " how the devil could
I mistake you for anybody else ? You were standing

on the rails between Tubby Waterhouse and little Jimmy O'Connor, and I have the most distinct recollection of every particular of the transaction."

And this had really been my position on the rails, which made the affair the more mysterious and awkward for me, for I was obliged to admit this fact, which served to confirm the worthy baronet in his illusion, for an illusion I knew it was. I perceived that nothing now would move him, so I left him and went back to my place in the ring, where a very agreeable surprise awaited me, and a revelation made which I have often thought of since those days, and one which I have always considered reflected infinite credit on Messrs. Shakeshaft & Clowes. To make a short story of it it appeared that this firm had laid Sir John the bet in question, and had honourably come forward the moment they learned of the claim being made upon me. I had always considered Walter Shakeshaft a rather good-looking fellow, and I felt flattered to be occasionally mistaken for him. In make and shape there was in those days some resemblance, and Sir John had evidently got us mixed up. However, he afterwards frankly admitted the error, and expressed his sorrow for the trouble he had given me.

" Still, it's a devilish good job for you, Dyke," he said, " you found the pea, for I could have sworn you laid me that bet."

Some months after, this was followed by a remarkable coincidence. During another settling a claim was made upon me for £100 on behalf of Lord Marcus Beresford.

I knew I had had no transaction with his lordship during the week, and at once told his agent so. Again I was assured I should have to pay, as it would no doubt be an error of mine, or of my clerk, Lord Beresford being too careful a man to make such a blunder. I felt very much annoyed and sorry; and while I felt certain it was his lordship's mistake, as I had no remembrance of even seeing him during the previous week, I knew that he was not only careful but one of the most upright of all swells I did business with, and, like jolly Sir John, he had a genial manner and a kindly word for everybody; and for one in my position it was most disagreeable to have disputes with such people.

It was agreed that the matter should stand over until I had an opportunity of speaking with his lordship, which opportunity came a few days after at Kempton Park.

"What the dickens do you mean, Master Dyke, by disputing that bet of mine?" his lordship inquired, as he came up to me between the races.

"I simply mean, my lord, that it was some one else you had that bet with, it certainly was not with me," I replied.

"Not you!" he answered with more sternness than I thought it possible his pleasant face could assume. "Why, I have as clear a recollection of the matter as though it had occurred two minutes ago. I was on the stand alongside Sir George Chetwynd, who had his glasses watching the start. He saw my horse had got a flying start, and you shouted out the name of the horse loudly offering to lay a hundred to ten against him. I shouted down to you, ' I'll take that ! ' You looked up at me, and replied, ' All right ' ; and then I saw you turn round to your clerk, who appeared to be putting the bet down. This I will swear to."

" I can only repeat, my lord, that it was not with me you had that bet," I said, and then a happy thought struck me.

" Will your lordship oblige me by walking down the side of the rails and have a good look at every one of the fielders ? " I asked.

" Certainly, if that will be any satisfaction to you," he answered.

And away we marched, Lord Beresford carefully scrutinising every one. When he came to Walter Shake-shaft he made a long pause, and I saw a puzzled look creep into his face.

" By Jove ! I begin to think you'll be right, my boy," he said ; then turning to Shakeshaft inquired, " Did I have a hundred to ten, a winner, of you last week, Shakeshaft ? "

" Yes, you did, my lord, and Clowes has just been telling me it was not claimed on Monday."

" Well, I'll never be certain about anything else," said his lordship, " for I would have gone upon my oath I had that bet with Master Dyke," and, turning to me, like the gentleman he was, he apologised for the trouble he had given me. So happily ended another incident which had looked for a time like being a very awkward one for me.

The frankness of his lordship and the jovial baronet's acknowledgment of his error contrast forcibly with a similar case which occurred at Stockbridge about the same time, in which case, if I remember rightly, one of the brothers Collins and Christy were concerned. Here a wrong claim was made by a swell of quite another sort, and on being referred to the committee of Tattersall's was promptly decided in favour of the swell; Collins being ordered to pay the captain forthwith, which he did while smarting under the certainty that he was being robbed of the money. Now, in this case also, Mr. Christy, who had laid the bet, was discovered and refunded the amount to Collins.

This fact was brought to the knowledge of the captain in the hope that he might be a gentleman as well as a captain, and be made to unsay some of the hard words he had used, and possibly in a mild sort of way, apologise for the wrong he had done. Nothing of the sort, however, happened; indeed quite the contrary. The captain more than insinuated that it was a got-up job among them to square themselves. This he could not really have believed. The fact was his was one of those spiteful little natures which could never forgive one he had wronged, or one who had proved his fallibility. There are a good many of this sort to be met with on the turf; but as a rule they do not belong to the blue-blooded aristocracy, but rather to shoddy specimens of it—the sons of men who have made their money in trade, and who are never guilty of referring to their grandfathers.

Before I close this chapter I must relate a very curious and, for the lookers-on, a most amusing case, which I think may also be called one of mistaken identity. It must be forty years ago, perhaps more, I was returning from a Midland race-meeting in a third-class carriage, with about half-a-dozen other turfites. In one corner of the carriage sat a thick-set, bullet-headed individual, the very type of a Brummagem bruiser, which one might easily have taken him to be, were it not for his clerical dress, the black broadcloth suit of the regulation cut, and the orthodox white choker. He had quietly ensconced himself in one of the corners, taking not the slightest notice of any of his fellow-travellers, excepting, perhaps, just to turn up the whites of his rather striking eyes when, occasionally, the language of two of the travellers became very violent and unnecessarily indecent; for the presence of the clergyman, so far from acting as a restraint upon these gentlemen, only seemed to increase their bad behaviour. After a little time the reverend gentleman fell into a gentle dose, or he feigned to do so. And then the fun began. Now these two men were in a fairly good position in the town they hailed from, and they would have considered themselves insulted to have been classed with the common rough, one being a prosperous shopkeeper and the other a well-known maltster. The latter was known also as a terrible bully, especially when it happened, as on the present occasion, he was exhilarated with an extra glass or two; and he had the reputation, moreover, of being useful with his fists. No sooner was the clergyman asleep, or apparently so, than they began playing practical jokes on him. One, getting his pipe into a welding heat, blew clouds of smoke into his face, and the other untied his choker. The parson seemed to sleep through these and similar jokes, perfectly oblivious to all his surroundings. The two ruffians, seeing these mild jokes had so little effect, proceeded to some of a more violent and indecent character. Whereupon, suddenly, the reverend gentleman opened his remarkable eyes, and at the same time tightly closed his immense fists, and like a flash of lightning his left went straight for the nose of the greengrocer, and, at the same instant, his right seriously disfigured a useful, but too prominent, organ of the maltster. Then followed a perfect storm of blows. To defend themselves was out of the question; they were no sooner on their feet than they were sent sprawling again as with a sledge-hammer; and in the space of about five minutes the two cowardly bullies got a well-deserved thrashing from the sturdy little parson. My travelling companions seemed struck with amazement, but to me the catastrophe caused no surprise; indeed, I felt certain I knew what would happen when those practical jokes commenced, for I had recognised in the clergyman my old friend, the invincible Birmingham pugilist, Morris Roberts, who at that time had one of his preaching fits on.

This story of Morris Roberts reminds me of another

also concerning one of the best known of the old Brummagem " fancy."

George Giles, better known as " Fat Un," was not one of Birmingham's most distinguished or most polished exponents of the noble art, but he was known far and wide as a terrible slogger, who could give and take as much punishment as any of his townsmen. I remember him well, and knew him in his palmiest days. A roly-poly sort of young fellow, thick-set, with a fat face, and an evident predisposition to adiposity. I remember when he gave over fighting, instead of taking a public-house and drinking himself to death, as so many of them do, he got himself converted by the Methodists ; went into business on his own account as a gasfitter, and settled down into a really quiet, harmless, and respectable member of society. His natural love of sport took the form of angling, and he became a devoted follower of the " Gentle Izaak." One day three Brummagem roughs were spending a day in the country, and, after their kind, were ready for any bit of devilment. In this frame of mind they came across a respectable-looking gentleman, rather stout, with a benevolent, florid face, and middle-aged, on the bank of the river, fishing. Here, evidently, was safe game for three sportive young men. One of them had the small branch of a tree in his hand ; he commenced the proceedings by shying it at the line, and so successfully, the fat gentleman was left with the rod in his hands, but line and float had gone. The fisherman mildly remonstrated.

" Why should you take such a liberty with me, young man ? " he asked. " I have done no harm to you, but it would serve you right to pitch you into the river after my line."

I dare say Mr. Giles—for he it was—had some idea what the effect of this threat would be, and, gentle as he was, would be prepared for it. Rough No. 1, using very bad language, threatened to throw the fat man after his line if he did not keep a civil tongue in his head, and came menacingly close up to him. Like a shot from a gun-barrel and straight from the shoulder, Mr. Giles let him have one of the old sort, and the young man was flat on his back, and considerably dazed. Almost at the same instant Rough No. 2 met with the same fate, while No. 3, realising that there had been a mistake somewhere, made off with all speed, leaving the local preacher and sometime pugilist, master of the field, and with an excellent opportunity of " improving the occasion," which, I believe, he did not neglect.

CHAPTER XIX

Old-fashioned welshers—My early experience of them—Johnny
  Quin—" The Captain " and the Tyke

I HAVE often wondered what could be the derivation of
the word " welsher " as applied among betting men.
I have heard many, but none which has seemed to me
perfectly satisfactory. A friend whom I have just
consulted on the subject says there is no doubt it was
suggested by the old rhyme commencing

" Taffy was a Welshman, Taffy was a thief."

But I am not prepared to accept this derivation
either, and am afraid my friend has allowed his judgment to be warped by prejudice, after a prolonged resi-
dence in private apartments at a fashionable Welsh water-
ing-place, where they kept a cat, or, I should say, a great
many cats. However difficult it may be to find the
derivation of the word, many of my readers will experience
no difficulty in supplying its definition ; for they have had,
in the course of their racing experiences, practical illus-
trations of it. I don't suppose the word welshing has
any great antiquity, but the practice is as old as gambling
of any sort ; and it has not been confined to the turf.

A form of welshing was very common 150 years ago, during the insane rage for lotteries. Of course, many of these gambling schemes were genuine enough, and among the millions of blanks some were fortunate enough to draw prizes of immense value. But those systems had their blacklegs and welshers. It was no uncommon thing for lottery offices to be opened, and after receiving money from great numbers of poor dupes, the managers, as they were called, would do " a guy," just as we have seen the same class act on racecourses in the present day. Sometimes, however, instead of levanting and closing the office in this sudden manner, they would conduct a bogus draw, in which the prizes would be so ridiculously out of proportion to the blanks they frequently led to riots, and sometimes loss of life.

My very earliest personal experience of betting on horse-racing has, doubtless, been the lot of many of my readers. My first acquaintance with a welsher was when a youth. I found myself at a race-meeting ; I knew nothing of race-horses, or jockeys, but I had half-a-crown in my pocket, so made up my mind to invest it, and as the jockeys paraded their horses in front of the Grand Stand, for lack of better judgment I selected the one I considered wore the prettiest jacket, and planked down my half-crown on him. Of course, it was a most silly thing to do, but, as luck would have it, this horse won at five to one. According to my hazy method of calculation, I made out there was twelve and sixpence coming from the bookie to whom I had confided my half-crown.

Don't laugh, gentle reader, I have seen the same mistake made many times, since those days, by much older and cleverer people. However, I went back gleefully to the spot where I left my bookie and my half-crown ; but the bland-looking, elderly person, with the black surtout coat and shiny top-hat, was nowhere to be seen. He'd been shouting a good deal, and I thought that, probably, he was dry and had gone to get a drink, so, unsuspecting guile in such a gentlemanly-looking elderly person, I waited with composure his return ; but when I found the numbers up for the next race and the betting in full swing again, I began to think I must have come to the wrong shop ; so I moved away in search of my bookie. During my ramble round the outside of the enclosure— on the opposite side to where I had made my bet—I came across a man with a remarkable family likeness to the gentleman, only he was wearing a light jacket with blue stripes and a white hat. Still, feeling confident he was my man, I made for him and demanded my twelve and sixpence. He simply said, in an indignant tone :

" Go away, sir ! What do you mean ? "

But before I could explain my meaning, I was hustled away by a couple of roughish-looking men.

" You've bin welshed, ain't you ? " asked one of these gentlemen.

" Well, I don't know what you mean by welshed," I replied ; " but I backed the last winner with that gentleman for half-a-crown, and I want my money."

" Look 'ere," the man said, " did the joker wot bet

R

wi' yo wear a black coort like a parson, and a shiny black
top-hat ? " This I was obliged to confess was so. " Theer
ye are agen," he said, turning appealingly to his companion ; " dain't I tell yer the d—d old thief was at his
games agen ! " Then to me, he continued : " The feller
wot did yo is that other gent's brother ; yo cum to-morrer
an' we'll find 'im for yer. Ye mustn't 'inder that gent in
'is busniss, or yo'll get locked up."

I didn't find it convenient to " cum to-morrer ; "
indeed, it was a good many years before I was able to
attend Wolverhampton—or, for the matter of that, any
other—race-meeting.

Welshing during my time has had three distinct periods,
each marked with characteristics peculiar to itself. From
earliest recollections of the turf up to about 1872, welshing
was a very mild sort of thing, and its professors were, for
the most part, rather elderly men, with a dejected, seedy
and out-of-elbows sort of look about them. I don't
believe it was generally a flourishing sort of business.
There was no organised ruffianism, such as we thereafter
became so familiar with ; indeed, there was no union of
any sort among them ; consequently little strength. When
one of these mean sneaks secured a few pounds he was
only too anxious to be off with it, thinking himself lucky
if he escaped a cruel pummelling at the hands of an
enraged crowd, or a ducking in the nearest water.

They were mostly a quiet, inoffensive set of men, and
but for their thieving propensities, quite harmless.

As far as observation goes, I don't think many of the

" chosen people " have gone astray in this direction, for these wary gentlemen the game was never good enough —but I am sorry to record the fact that I remember one sheenie welsher, and I dare say there are some old racing men who will remember him better than I do. He was a big dark man, with a most pronounced Semitic cast of face, and a stoop in his shoulders ; with the appearance of having in some part of his life lost something he was for ever seeking. Like his friend and contemporary, Manning, he wore a quiet, almost sad expression ; and while perhaps not the most desirable of characters yet one of the endurable parasites of racing. He was called " big Nathan."

An equally well-known old traveller in the same line was poor old Johnny Quin. I have frequently heard him called " the honest welsher," I suppose the adjective being used here in the comparative sense. It was not that he refrained from plunder where he had the opportunity, or that he was ever known, willingly, to repay the victims he had robbed ; but I have known highly respectable members of the ring lend him half-a-sovereign to go to a race-meeting or to help him home again after an unsuccessful meeting, and these amounts he never failed to repay. One good-hearted—albeit, perhaps indiscreet—bookie, poor Will Knee, frequently Johnny's banker, was soundly abused for this practice.

" Ah well, we've all to live," he would say, " so has this poor old devil ; he lives on the involuntary contributions of the new mugs. How many of us are doing the same in a different way ? Good luck to him ! "

I have said that these old-fashioned welshers were almost a harmless set of men. Compared with the class which succeeded them, they were honest gentlemen. They were mostly very poor, and I have often thought they were welshers less from choice than necessity.

The most notable example of the class I have hitherto written of was a man known for many years as " the Captain," and by this name only shall he be known here ; not only because he lived to occupy a far different position on the turf and in commercial life, but because he has left behind him some who have inherited the better traits of his character. Of this singular type of his class I shall now have to speak.

The Captain was known, wherever there was racing, all over England ; and, taking him altogether, his was the most interesting personality which has ever appeared on the turf in the shape of a welsher. In personal appearance he was a remarkable man ; he was thick-set and rather above the average height ; his face, although badly pock-marked, indicated considerable shrewdness and natural intelligence ; his eyes, small, keen, and restless, like those of a bird of prey, were always on the look-out for victims ; he wore his iron-grey hair cropped short as with a clipping machine ; he made up for this, however, by cultivating a splendid moustache of the same colour. In his bearing he affected the high military style of which he was uncommonly proud, and which, doubtless, had secured him his nickname. In his manner he was suave and gentle, and polite almost to excess, and he exercised, in the practice of his despicable calling, a patient perseverance, industry, and ability which—applied in a more legitimate course—might have secured him a big position in life. As it was, they got for him several rows of houses, and with them a certain sort of consideration and respect, which the world always concedes to wealth, or reputed wealth, and to success—however achieved.

The Captain was, indeed, the only one of the welshers belonging to his school who got money and saved it. To begin with, he had more ability than his fellows ; and what even more than this accounted for it, was the fact of his being a steady, sober sort of fellow, with the one fixed idea, never to " part "—for any purpose, or to any person—when he had once secured a bit. I have heard him confess that, in his early days, he seldom went through the formality of taking a railway ticket to the towns he was intending to honour with his presence ; and as he was never burdened with superfluous personal luggage he frequently managed to dispense with the necessity for unpleasant leave-takings with indulgent hosts and hostesses ; and as for admittance to the various race-course enclosures, I am not aware that the clerks of courses supplied him with complimentary tickets, but I am quite certain he never paid for admission.

He was in the habit of leaving his home, bound for a race-meeting, with no money at all, or next to none, and every night, without fail, whatever sums he had been able to put his " thieving irons " on, much or little, and by whatever means obtained, it was turned into post office orders and despatched home, so that if it should happen that he got caught and " turned up," there was but small chance of recovering anything from this astute practitioner.

" They might tear the clothes off my back," I have heard him say, " there was always some benevolent farmer or sympathetic village tradesman ready to rig me out with a better suit. They might duck me in the pond and cudgel me till I was half dead, but I had always the consolation of knowing that the money was safely at home."

It was very amusing to hear him tell, in after years, of the toil and hardships he endured, the cruelties he occasionally suffered at the hands of enraged mobs, and the ingenious tricks he practised to elude the enemy. It was, as a rule, hazardous business to take on Yorkshiremen, and the Captain had a wholesome fear of the tykes. They were not only keen on the welsher, but when they caught one they were apt to be inconsiderate and brutally vindictive ; indeed, they have been known, on more than one or two occasions, to handle them in such a way as to leave them of little service as welshers —or in any other capacity—thereafter ; and I believe, from what he said, the worthy Captain had himself suffered at the hands of these stubborn and unforgiving Yorkshiremen. However, he ventured to Doncaster on a certain St. Leger week, when so many favourites were beaten every day that he found himself able to remain in the ring all four days; and so successful had he been in finding " flats " he had despatched quite a nice little parcel every night to his excellent wife at the Metropolis of the Midlands, where she resided. Toward the end of the business on the last day, he managed to lay a gentleman twenty pounds to five against a two to one chance, which was decidedly indiscreet, because it had the effect of making the punter suspicious; so, without the Captain knowing it, he kept his eye on him, and made up his mind to resist the temptation to see the race, in order to be able to do so. But before it was over—in fact, before the horses were at the post—the Captain left his place, and leisurely made for the exit gate; having cast a furtive glance on all sides to make sure none of his clients were within sight. None of them were in sight, so he was considerably surprised when an instant after the Yorkshireman was at his side, as though he had sprung out of the earth armed, like a certain example in mythology.

" What bist t'after ? " inquired the tyke, glaring savagely at him.

" All right, my boy, I'm not going to run away," cheerfully answered the Captain; " come with me if you're frightened."

So the tyke followed him to a part of the ring which was pretty clear of the crowd. When there, he turned his back on the Yorkshireman, and appeared to be counting his bank. In the meantime the horses had started, and very soon, unluckily for the welsher, the tyke's horse won. Whatever sensations of fear and anxiety may have possessed the gallant Captain at that moment he didn't permit his face to betray, but turning lightly to his companion he said :

" Look here, my friend, I've had a very bad day, and I find I haven't enough with me to settle with you ; but it will be all right, I assure you. Just jump into a cab with me. I've plenty down at my lodging, and I'll pay you honourably ; I'm no welsher, I assure you," and his high military bearing, combined with his gentlemanly and persuasive language, was too much for the poor tyke. Scarcely daring to doubt, yet feeling slightly uncomfortable, he went off with the Captain, who chartered a hansom, and was soon on the way to his lodgings. He pulled up at a respectable-looking little house near the Turf Tavern. The tyke was about to pay the cabby and discharge him.

" I'll see to him," says the Captain ; " he can wait a few minutes while I have a cup of tea, and you must have one with me while you're here, and then he can drive me, with my luggage, down to the station." This all looked so straightforward that the tyke was made much easier in his mind.

" Here, missus," cried the Captain to the good woman of the house, who was in the little back kitchen by herself, " I'm back a bit earlier than I expected, and I've brought a friend with me ; get a cup of tea for us, sharp, while I go upstairs and put my things together."

This he proceeded to do, while the good woman busied about the sitting-room, laying the table for her lodger and his friend. Now the cunning Yorkshireman, as he came in, had noticed an entry at the side of the house, and while now relieved of much of the doubt which had before possessed him, he thought he wouldn't throw a chance away, so, as the Captain went upstairs, he slipped out to the cabman.

" Look here, cabby," says he, " an' tha sees yon chap come doon 'tentry just call me oot of t'house, and I'll pay th' well for it." Then he slipped as quickly into the house again and waited for the Captain to join him at tea, and pay him the twenty-five pounds. The table was laid, the tea was " mashed," the bread and butter ready, a bit of cold meat, the remnant of the Captain's dinner, on the table ; but the Captain tarried so long the tyke became anxious, and the old woman rather alarmed. At last she impatiently hammered the stairs with the haft of her bread-knife, screaming out at the top of her voice, " Th' tay be ready, sir ; thou'lt have it cold ! "

There was no response, and no sound of movement in the room above. The Yorkshireman could bear the suspense no longer, so he joined the old lady in the kitchen.

" Hadn't you better go up to his rooms and see what he's after ? " said he, a dreadful suspicion coming over him.

The old woman acted upon his suggestion, knocking

violently at the door; still there was no response. She
tried to open the door; it was locked. Then she began to
scream. She knew, she said, the gent had been and made
away with himself because he'd lost his money at the races.
The tyke had been already more than half disposed to
that opinion, and when the cabman assured him he had
neither come down the entry or through the window that
way, he felt horrified with the certainty of it. What was
to be done? They were dumb with the horror and fear
of it. A little knot of neighbours had now collected, and
some one proposed they should either break open the
bedroom door or fetch a policeman who would do it. So
cabby was sent in search of an officer, and after a time,
having succeeded, the door was burst open, and the
Yorkshireman with two or three of the bolder spirits
followed the policeman into the room, prepared to be
still further horrified. They found, however, no indica-
tion of a dreadful suicide; no man was in the room, dead
or alive. There was a dilapidated old papier mâché port-
manteau not worth carrying away, and that was all that
remained of the Captain. The active and intelligent
officer, after looking up the chimney and under the bed,
turned quite savagely upon those about him, demanding
to know why he had been fooled in this manner. The
door had been locked on the outside and the key carried
away. This was evidently a manœuvre to gain time while
he secured his retreat worthy the military reputation of
my hero. After the officer had made a careful examination of the premises, inside and outside, he began to cross-

question the cabby, more than insinuating that he had either allowed himself to go for a little nap, or over to the Turf Tavern for a little drink, and so permitted the man to escape. The poor cabby, exasperated at this imputation upon his honour and truthfulness, swore, as only cabbies can swear; declaring he had neither closed an eye nor moved from the spot, so that he couldn't have escaped down the entry. It remained for a sharp lad, instead of an active and intelligent officer, to discover an altogether different and easy means of escape, which was, after all, ridiculously obvious. This was a low wall which formed the boundary of the little yard, over which a person might almost step into a similar little yard, and thence down another entry leading to a street running parallel to ours.

By this means, and while the busy housewife had been laying the table for two, had the Captain escaped, and he was now on the way to Birmingham, hugging himself complacently after another brilliant victory; doubtless amusing himself as to what the old woman would say when she found he had taken his departure without the usual formality; and what cabby would charge the Yorkshireman for his exciting job.

The remarkable strategy and resourcefulness of the gallant Captain in this episode clearly qualify him as a general among welshers; his grasp of the situation, determination, and courage, were characteristic of the man, and worthy a better cause.

There can be but little doubt had the daring spirit, clear-sightedness, energy, and other qualities, which went to make the bold welsher what he was, been exercised in any legitimate business, he would have been a notably successful man. This would appear to have been the opinion of a number of people besides myself, and it was not an uncommon thing to hear the expression of this opinion. One gentleman held it so firmly, he decided to back it by risking a considerable sum of money. This was Mr. William Taylor, who, with his brother George, were well-known bookmakers, hailing from the Emerald Isle. These gentlemen were devout Catholics, and were both of them among the most straightforward and bene-volent men I ever met with. Will Taylor, being impressed as I said with the evident ability of the Captain, deter-mined upon the Quixotic task of his reclamation. The Captain's plausible tongue had almost convinced him that it was only want of means which had prevented him shining in some straight way long before; indeed, it would appear it had been by the merest chance he hadn't been a saint instead of a welsher.

"Supposing I start you with a small bank to begin with," said Mr. Taylor, "will you promise me to bet fair and go straight?"

"I should think I would, Mr. Taylor," the Captain replied. "Why, it's the opportunity I've been waiting for and longing for all my life."

"Then you shall start to-morrow at Warwick," said the philanthropist. "I'll provide the necessary tools, and be behind you to the extent of a hundred pounds to begin with; and I'll make people acquainted with the fact as far as possible, so you may be able to get a little betting."

With tears of gratitude welling up in his eyes, and loud in praise of his benefactor, the Captain took his departure ; and on the following day behold him in the ring at Warwick, equipped and eager to commence his new career as a legitimate layer, declaring on his honour to Mr. Taylor, and to all whom it might concern, that nothing on earth should make him go crooked again if Mr. Taylor would only stand by him. Well, the first race being over, the philanthropist, full of excitement, rushes off to see how the new bookie has fared.

"Well, Captain, what have you done ? " asked he. But he need scarcely have asked ; the Captain's beaming countenance proclaimed the good news, "a skinner" to begin with, which was set down as an augury of good. A clear book for £27 gave him heart to bet even more vigorously on the second race ; and he was rewarded by even better results ; he had yet another clear book for nearly £40. Again Taylor hurried up to the "joint," and the Captain almost embraced him in his effusive gratitude.

"Oh, what have I been doing all these years ? " he exclaimed. " I've been at the wrong game, I can see. Why, if I'd only gone straight long ago, I should have been a rich man now."

Taylor, seeing things going so well, and feeling sincerely anxious to help on the good work as much as possible, now recommended some of his friends, who punted in small amounts to do business with him, vouching for his honesty, and even going as far as to have himself a few bets with him. So on the third race his betting had so much increased that another " skinner " resulted in a win of upwards of £60. This made him about a hundred and thirty to the good, and gave rise to visions of rows of nice-looking houses to be called " Straight Villas," with an industrious penciller collecting the rents.

The result of the fourth race, alas ! demonstrated the futility of human hopes, and knocked the " baseless fabric " of the Captain's dreams all of a heap, for it produced a low, selfish sort of punter, with no desire, like Taylor, for the reclamation of an erring Captain ; and this man had the ill-grace to put a tenner on the winner, and as it was a large field, although favourite, it started at three to one, so that this inconsiderate punter was entitled to £40. Mr. Taylor, of course, expected there would be a loss on this race, so promptly made for the spot where the Captain had selected as his " pitch." He was rather surprised to find instead of his gallant friend, one of the punters whom he had guaranteed waiting to draw £40. You may perhaps better imagine than I can describe his feelings when he found the numbers up for the next race, and no Captain. Indeed, the pitch was " to let " for the remainder of the meeting. He had intended returning to Ireland after Warwick, but the conduct of his protegée so vexed his philanthropic soul, he remained in England, travelling about from meeting to meeting, for several weeks, in the hope of meeting with the ungrateful welsher. After about a month, he suddenly came across him at another Midland meeting; and, so far from trying to avoid him, the gallant Captain put on his high military style, saluting his friend and would-be regenerator with the boldest effrontery.

" You're a nice sort of fellow," began Taylor; " nice sense of honour or gratitude you must have to treat a man as you have treated me. You rascal! You ought to be whipped off the face of the earth."

" Come, come, Mr. Taylor; draw it mild," the Captain replied. " I was really obliged to bolt at Warwick."

" Obliged to bolt! How so ? " asked Mr. Taylor.

" They backed the winner," answered the inveterate welsher, looking astonished that any human being should be weak enough to expect him to remain at his post under such circumstances.

" How much had you to pay the winner ? " asked the philanthropist.

" About £60," was the reply; " and if I'd paid him I should have had to part with all I'd had the trouble of collecting on that race, and about £15 of my previous winnings. I couldn't do it—I really couldn't, Mr. Taylor."

" Yes, but didn't I tell you I would be by your side," said that gentleman, " and if you required it, find the money ? "

The irredeemable old scamp sighed deeply and in quite pathetic tones replied :

" It's no use talking, Mr. Taylor; I tell you I couldn't pull it out again. I didn't think it possible I could get

£60 back again that afternoon, as there were only two more races ; and as the punters had begun finding winners, I thought they might perhaps go on doing it."

The high-principled and generous Irishman, recognising the incorrigible character of the creature upon whom he had wasted his humane efforts, and feeling that nothing he might say or do would have the slightest effect upon him, let him go his way, only registering mentally a solemn vow that he would be guilty of no more Quixotic feats of knight-errantry on behalf of fallen humanity in the shape of confirmed old welshers.

For several years after this the Captain continued his welshing career ; but he was becoming an old man, and he had lost much of his old dash and daring. And his soul revolted at the brutal methods of the new school of welshers which was just springing into existence. He had invested some money in a commercial undertaking and that looked like meeting with considerable success ; but it didn't go well with his old occupation. But after all, I do believe the factor which most strongly influenced him in his decision to relinquish his nefarious profession was an intense yearning to mingle in good society ; to meet on equal footing men of position and respectability, who had been in the habit of looking upon him and his occupation with contempt. To attain this purpose there was nothing he would not do ; he would grovel in the dust or spend and lose his dearly-loved and hardly-earned money like the veriest " mug." He succeeded in this object as he did in most of the matters he set his mind upon ; but the price he paid for the distinction he coveted was out of all proportion to its value, and will scarcely be believed by those unacquainted with the latter part of his history, and who only remember him as the hard-headed and shrewd old welsher.

Two or three years after the relinquishment of his profession of welsher he reappeared on the field of former glories in the character of a gentleman backer ; and so adroitly did he manage matters, he was soon " taken on " by most of the leading pencillers of the ring and was found betting to a considerable amount of money, with an account every week at the clubs and at Tattersall's. He became possessed of an intense desire to become a member of one of the best and most respectable sporting clubs in the country. At first he failed in this attempt ; but with astute management and after what he called " indomitable *per-sev-ver-ance*," his numerous efforts were crowned with success. At most of the clubs just at this time there was a rage for high play at cards, and the game of baccarat was the one most in vogue. The club I have referred to was no exception to the rule, and no sooner had the Captain become a member than he was seized with a mania for baccarat ; and night after night when he was not away racing he might be found, eager-eyed and earnest, doing battle with the fates at the baize-covered table.

Fate was not kind to him—perhaps it resented his desertion of a profession wherein it had secured for him so much profit and renown—and now like a very butcher

s

it had the knife in him. In his own line he never had an equal; at this green-table he was a child contending with men. Anyway he lost heavily and nearly constantly. He couldn't give it up—it had become a mania with him; he almost lived at the club; and the play had got to be a necessary part of his existence. It was known that monkeys had settled on the roofs of all his rows of houses. Trying to recover what he was losing at cards he began to bet heavier and recklessly at racing, with the inevitable result that there came a Monday when the Captain's racing account was missing, and he found himself obliged to retire from his beloved club in an absolutely ruined condition. Poor old Captain! I saw him many times after that, walking about in complete poverty; reduced to lying in wait for the pals of his better days in order to beg the means for a dinner. He was now too old and broken in spirit to make fresh attempts to raise himself from this condition. To return to the only mode of life in which he had been successful was out of the question; and if he had attempted it he would certainly have failed. Welshing had undergone a complete change; its methods would have disgusted the Captain's suave and gentlemanly spirit, and it would have been impossible for him to have mixed with its then turbulent professors; clearly welshing had become an impossibility for him. The friends and acquaintances of his prosperous days naturally enough gave him the cold shoulder; indeed, treated him with the contempt which he deserved—deserved for being a fool and not a rogue; not because of a wasted and dishonourable life, full of low lying and thieving ; not because of splendid abilities perverted to vilest uses ; not even because he owed them anything or had done them personally any wrong, did they despise him, but simply because he was poor.

It was clear there were no possibilities, no place for him in this life, and nothing for him but to die.   This the poor old wretch did some fifteen years ago.   Of course I am not going to excuse or extenuate the execrable profession of welshing of any kind ; but I am bold to reiterate an opinion I have elsewhere pronounced—the Captain, with all his faults, was a gentleman compared with the vile wretches who succeeded him in the welshing profession ; about whom I shall have something to say in my next chapter.

CHAPTER XX

The brutal school of welshers—How I came by a limping gait—
The Battle of Ewell—" Punch " and his history

THE old-fashioned welshers of whom I have written are
an extinct race. They were not a credit to the turf,
but as I have said they were endurable parasites. They
fleeced the unwary and made the young beginner pay his
" footing " ; content to rob their victims and sneak off
with the plunder. The *modus operandi* was highly
interesting, and as I have shown, their trickiness and skill
in evading the enemy testified to rare natural abilities,
and often afforded amusement to those interested as
lookers-on. These comparatively innocent old welshers,
with their simple methods, were succeeded by what I
may style the dark ages of the turf, when welshers
" came not in a single file," but in whole battalions,
terrorising the ring and setting all lawful authorities at
defiance. It would seem as though the good news had
been conveyed to the purlieus of thievery in all our great
cities that here was a field of labour for the thief, where
to ply his occupation in broad daylight and in sight of the
very guardians of the law without fear of interference ;
nay, more than this, where they might be guaranteed the

protection of their old enemy " the copper," if they should have the misfortune to be caught and overpowered by those they were robbing.

Some of my readers, whose experience of the turf does not go back as far as these dark days, will discredit this description of matters and be inclined to charge me with exaggeration ; but it is strictly true, and any old racing man who lived through those days with his eyes open will endorse what I say. Many times I have seen these vagabonds caught in the act, and when their victims, taking the law into their own hands, were about to inflict a well-merited punishment, the policeman would step in to guard the thief, taking him into custody only to release him the moment he was perfectly safe. More than this, I have seen the welsher when pursued run into the arms of a police-man, demanding his protection, and getting it with the same result.

No wonder, then, that these people greatly increased in numbers, and as they went about in gangs became power-ful, and were indeed a terror not only to backers but to layers also. If a man had been plundered in the most cruel and barefaced manner, the advice generally offered by his experienced friends in the ring was, " You had better put up with it. It's more than one's life is worth to interfere with them."

Welshers were not only thieves, they were composed of the very residuum of thievery. No such blackguards and irredeemable ruffians would ever have been permitted to follow their nefarious occupation for such a length of time in any other civilised country under the sun.   The brigandage of Italy in its worst times was nothing to it, and if it had been allowed to continue and grow to the present day it would have put a stop to racing.   Indeed it was only when it menaced the very existence of the sport that steps were taken to check it, and all honour is due to the magistrates at Ascot who so construed an Act of Parliament as to warrant them in sending welshers to prison, which aforetime had never been done ; thus creating a precedent which many magistrates have since followed, to the purification of the turf in a remarkable degree.

Some of my readers may incline to the opinion that I have overdrawn the picture and am unduly severe on welshers of the period under notice.   I answer that exaggerations were almost impossible, and personal experience warrants me—if excuse were necessary—in the use of the strongest language at command.   I owe it to the unspeakable brutality and ruffianism of these thieves that I have gone maimed and limping through nearly forty years of my life, and which I shall do through all that remains of it, knowing no day in all the years, and but few hours, without more or less of pain.   It is therefore natural that I should feel bitterly, and say what I feel.   At the same time I know that there are thousands of racing men who would bear witness that I have not spoken a bit too strongly against these cowardly pests of the turf.

I cannot better illustrate their character, and the

condition to which the ring was reduced in the early seventies, than by giving " a round, unvarnished tale," of my sufferings at the hands of welshers.

I was betting in the ring at Brighton, in partnership with W. Knee, who was till recently one of the most widely known starting price merchants in the provinces. I was betting, and my young friend was booking. Up came a man who will be remembered as Big Fisher, one of the most notable scoundrels of the gang then travelling ; he took £10 to £5 the favourite, posting with me his £5. After he had turned away, my partner remarked :

" If this favourite wins, I shall want you to stop a tenner he welshed me of at Worcester."

" That was before you joined me," I answered ; " and, of course, has nothing to do with me. But if he wins, and you intend stopping it, you had better take the money, and settle with him when he comes."

As the favourite won, I awaited with some anxiety the return of Fisher, knowing him for one of the most violent and dangerous of all the thieving fraternity. It was not long before he put in an appearance, and my partner handed him his fiver back, which was all he considered due.

" What does this mean ? " inquired the ruffian.

" It means that I've stopped the tenner you owe me for Worcester," replied my friend.

The welsher, foaming with rage, dashed the money on the ground with a volley of the most fearful oaths, and at once went for my partner, who was then a well-built, powerful young fellow, nearly as heavy as Big Fisher. In an instant a crowd was around them, composed very largely of " the boys," and all was confusion. The combatants were on the ground together, and it was clear that Fisher, unaided, would fare badly ; but the thief was not to go unaided, for I distinctly saw one of his pals, a fellow named, or nicknamed, " Butcher," deliberately kick at Knee while they were on the ground. This was a bit more than I could stand, so I rushed in and pulled Butcher away. The fight was, of course, soon over, as the police were near at hand ; but I have painful reasons for remembering the diabolical expression on Mr. Butcher's face as he turned away from me, saying :

" Look after yourself, you—— ——. We'll do you next. We know you're a —— policeman."

The latter remark, I afterwards learned, referred to my acquaintance with the celebrated Scotland Yard detective, Tanner, with whom they had seen me talk occasionally, although, on no occasion, had they or their doings been the subject of conversation.

Well, I thought the matter had blown over, at any rate for the present, and was just beginning to bet on the following race, when a little fellow came hurriedly past me, and, without looking at me, earnestly whispered, " Keep your eyes open, the boys are on you," or words to that effect. I turned to look after the would-be friend, and as I did so received a fearful blow on the side of the head ; in a second I was on the ground, being kicked all over. I was literally surrounded by the ruffians ; but I well remember seeing among my assailants Big Fisher, Butcher, and a dreadful thief from Birmingham named Sam Unwin. In two minutes, and before assistance could reach me, I was fearfully mauled. Among other injuries, my leg was broken in the ankle, and the joint dreadfully dislocated, the muscles being so badly lacerated as to preclude the possibility of ever becoming sound again.

I was carried to my lodgings in the King's Road, suffering excruciating pains, and there I lay for many weeks. In the meantime, articles had appeared, anent the subject, in various newspapers ; a sort of committee, composed of a few well-known members of the ring, took the question up, and warrants were issued for the arrest of such of the miscreants as I was able to identify. They, however, left the country or kept out of the way for a long time ; and the following year the matter was allowed to drop. I had all along made up my mind that neither I nor any one individual ought to be singled out for the purpose of prosecuting these villains, not only because I knew the danger to the individual, but I felt it ought to be undertaken by a body representing the whole ring, in the interests of the ring and of the public. Butcher, from what I afterwards saw of him, no doubt relinquished his disreputable calling ; anyway, I never remember to have seen him following it from that time. The other two, after my affair had blown over, continued their thieving career as boldly as ever, and I have known them more than once assisting at scenes as shameful as that described. They were both drunkards as well as thieves. Big Fisher dropped out of sight many years ago, and I should say he had either drunk himself to death or died doing time in one of His Majesty's prisons. The last time I saw Unwin, years ago, he was too old and emaciated to get about the country, so he was employed on Saturday nights outside a " cag-mag " meat shop in one of the low parts of Birmingham, touting for customers. Soon after this I heard of his dying in abject poverty in one of the slums of that city.

These men were not exceptions, they were fair samples of what welshers had now become, and the treatment I received was not more brutal than scores of respectable men underwent at the hands of these or other members of the fraternity.

At Lichfield, a year or two after my case, I witnessed a scene more horrible than that wherein I was concerned, because the victim was an elderly man, and apparently in a feeble condition. A firm of welshers had established themselves in the ring ; the ruffian who acted the part of bookmaker was perched on the top of a high stool. He had hung round his neck, by means of a broad yellow strap, a large satchel, on the front of which was emblazoned in gold letters the name of one of the best-known book-makers. This, by the by, was a very common practice, and in more than one case I have known respectable looking bookmakers permit their names to be forged in this way, and the public thereby gulled, because they were afraid of the consequences to themselves if they interfered.

Well, the respectable old gentleman I have referred to, it appeared, had deposited two sovereigns with the welsher, taking him £12 to that amount a certain horse which won, and, of course, he demanded of the thief, who had borrowed the straight man's name, the fourteen pounds he was entitled to. In the days of the old-fashioned welsher he would have found the " pitch " to let ; not so with the modern type of welsher, he maintained his position with an effrontery bred of constant success ; so the old man handed up his ticket.

" How much do you want ? " asked the welsher in the business-like manner of the straight man.

" £14, sir," replied the old gentleman.

" Number 725, £14," shouted the thief to his fellow-thief, who acted as his clerk, and who, after pretending to look at the book, looked innocently up at his master, remarking :

" The gentleman's put the wrong horse down ; he backed a loser," and the welsher tears up the ticket into little bits, and throws them into the old man's face.

" Go away, you old scamp," says he ; " what are you trying on ? "

Some old gentlemen would have gone away terrified at the savage demeanour of this bookmaker, supplemented as it was by the rude and uncomplimentary remarks of a little band of square-headed ruffians by whom he was immediately surrounded. But this old gentleman, with more valour than discretion, was not of that metal. He was an excitable and passionate little man, and he commenced a violent argument, and when he found himself being hustled about by those surrounding him he made a snatch at the satchel, which was the signal for " the boys " to begin their work. In about one minute the poor old man was kicked into unconsciousness, his pockets rifled of watch and money, and I have no doubt that, although no bones were broken, he had received injuries which would trouble him as long as he lived, and probably shorten his life. The welsher and his confederates got clear away to continue the like business elsewhere.

Occasionally these ruffians met with their due ; and once they did so, I remember, under amusing circumstances.

A few of my elderly readers will remember the famous Battle of Ewell, which was much talked about at the time.

A gang of welshers, hailing chiefly from Manchester, Nottingham, and Sheffield, and known as " The Forty," were very much in evidence in those days. A party of them, during the Epsom Summer Meeting, had quartered themselves at the pretty little village of Ewell, at whose capital old hostelry some of us rested many a time for a drink on the way. It is a few miles from the course, and on one of the highways to London ; and as in those times vast numbers of those attending the races went by road, it is easy to imagine, if you don't remember, what a busy place the little village was on " the Derby Day." A couple of the pleasant party I have named lodged at a cottage down one of the lanes, and after the labours of the day on the downs, hither they repaired for a good feed and unlimited booze. On the Derby Day in question after these two young men had so regaled themselves, they strolled into the main road and joined the crowds who were watching the carriage-loads of jovial folk returning from the races. Some will recognise the two men when I tell them they were known as Punch and Iron Mask. Punch was a cobby-built fellow, with a big head on broad shoulders, and a flat nose on a face as big, and about the colour, of an old-fashioned copper warming-pan. His pal was a much taller man, with a slight stoop, very long arms, and a cadaverous-looking face, with huge jaws and prominent cheek-bones, which almost obscured his wolfish little eyes. And they were both supposed to be able to scrap a bit; indeed, they were quite a terror to quiet folk, but, as is generally found to be the case with such, they were both, at bottom, arrant cowards.

They had no sooner taken their stand on the high ground forming the footpath on one side of the road than they proceeded to pelt the carriage people, passing by, with rotten eggs, sods of turf, and sundry other objectionable missiles; while other of the onlookers contented themselves with blowing peas through a tube, and less objectionable annoyances. Most of the passengers took it all as a matter of course, and bore it as became the day and the occasion. A carriage drawn by a pair of high-stepping horses was coming by, and a couple of young swells with two ladies, evidently of the blue blood, were seated in the carriage. Punch and his friend, in an unlucky moment, thinking this was an excellent opportunity for a little extra display, shied a huge sod, which caught one of the ladies on the head, sadly frightening her, and what was worse, utterly spoiling her headgear. This resulted in a surprising deviation from the usual state of things, and instead of the coachman having orders to drive faster, the horses were stopped suddenly, and out jumped the two young swells, and in an instant they were face to face with their ruffianly assailants, and the most remarkable part of the business was that the welshers immediately recognised in the two swells a couple of their victims on the course.

" You two blackguards will have to fight," began the shorter of the swells, " or else you will have to be locked up ; now, which is it to be ? "

" Hear, hear ! bravo, little 'un," shouted some of the bystanders, and it was clear there were enough honest Englishmen present to see fair play, and who, English like, dearly love to see a fight. The welshers blustered a bit to begin with, but seeing no way out of it, threw off their jackets, and prepared for the fray. " You take Mr. Flatnose," said the gentleman, who had spoken before, " and I'll have a go at this big thief who welshed me to-day."

The taller of the gentlemen protested against this arrangement, and wanted to slip into the big one, but the little one wouldn't hear of it, and so began the famous battle of Ewell.

As the two fights began at the same moment, it is rather difficult to describe the early stages of them. Punch was a Lancashire man, and believing if he could succeed in getting a grip of his opponent he would be able to trip him up and fall on him, according to the custom of the boys in his county ; and surmising at once that he should have no chance in ordinary fighting, immediately he stood before his opponent he made a dash to get hold, but instead of the gentleman he got hold of a blow straight from the shoulder, and delivered on Punch's poor flat nose with a force and precision which not only scored first blood for the gentleman, but made the bully's thick body spin, and his eyes strike fire, ere he flopped on the earth like a lump of lead.   When they picked him up he would have run if there had been any run left in him ; as it was, he had evidently had enough, and the men who had volunteered to second him had almost to throw him at his terrible enemy.   This time his attempt to rush the gentleman was of the feeblest description ; he was instantly seized by the scruff of the neck, and the swell held him there till he had sufficiently pummelled him, and then sent him reeling to mother earth.   The gentleman was satisfied, and Punch was more than satisfied and was glad to sneak away without inquiring after the fate of his pal.

Meanwhile, Iron Mask, having an immense advantage in size and the length of his reach, was not doing quite so badly as Punch, and that is all that can be said for him, for, despite the length of his reach, he had never been

able to touch his little opponent, who, in point of science
and condition, was as far in front of him as was Tom
Sayers to an untutored yokel, so he got peppered on nose,
and eyes, and high cheek-bones to such a purpose his wife
would never have known him.

It took something longer to bring this result about
than Punch's punishment had taken, but it was just as
effective, and before they had been at it many minutes
Iron Mask knew he had no chance whatever, so instead of
coming up to time, after a stinging thump in the ribs,
which had nearly knocked the life out of him, he quietly
turned his back, and was for slinking away after his friend
Punch.

" No, you don't go like that," said the gentleman,
following him up and taking hold of him. Iron Mask,
seeing him at such close quarters, suddenly turned round,
a very devil gleaming in his eyes, and letting fly at the
gentleman, caught him a nasty blow on the side of the
head. This naturally exasperated the swell, so he set
about him in earnest. Ding ! dong ! like sledge-hammers,
on ribs, mouth, and nose went the iron fists of the gentleman, till the big welsher was out of puff and utterly
cowed ; and again would have sought safety in flight.
" You don't move from here," said the plucky little swell,
dodging round him, but keeping a safe distance, " till you
apologise, and say you have had enough ; and if you
don't do so, I'll set about you again."

Anything was preferable to this, and he proceeded to
apologise in abject fashion, and declared, I am sure, with

more truthfulness than he was accustomed to use, that he had had enough, and only then was he allowed to follow his friend to the little cottage down the lane.

The two swells, who had not troubled to remove their coats, and as cool as though nothing had happened, proceeded down the road to where their carriage awaited them, and drove off amid the cheers of the crowd; and so ended the Battle of Ewell. Iron Mask has been dead many years; but it was only the other day that I came across Punch, within a few yards of one of the principal sporting clubs of London; a poor, shrivelled-up old wretch, ragged and bootless and hungry, lying in wait for sporting men, who, he had reason to know, have tender hearts, and stand the " whispering " of the most worthless objects, whose sole claim to charity is their poverty and bitter distress.

With varying fortune, for many years Punch continued his disreputable occupation. At times the buffets of the fickle goddess drove him into deep waters, and he met with rough usage at her hands. At other times he made heaps of money, lived on the fat of the land, and dressed like a swell; and there is no doubt what he tells me is perfectly true, if he had saved his earnings like " The Captain " he would now have been a man of fortune, with a charming villa in the suburbs of his native town; a respected member, perhaps a committeeman, of several important clubs, and an honoured pillar of various political associations. Who can tell? I have seen these honourable positions held by men made of no better material

T

than poor old Punch, men who lived for years by his
methods, or worse. Punch, like many a better man,
has missed his golden opportunities, and they will come
to him no more. For him there remains no honourable
offices, no charming country villa, but a painful pilgrimage to something quite different.

CHAPTER XXI

Laying against " safe 'uns "—The true story of the Fraulein
case—The disqualification of Pattern.

I HAVE told my readers already how disastrously some of
my early efforts at finding " safe 'uns," to lay against,
turned out ; and have made frank confession of a weakness in that respect, the like of which has, I believe,
afflicted every layer I have known, with one solitary
exception.

After I had improved my position, and was betting to a
large amount of money, I felt no less disposed to lay a bit
extra against a horse I knew, or thought I knew, had no
chance. All this I know, as well as you, dear reader, is
dreadfully immoral ; and I ought to be ashamed of myself
for such an unblushing confession. But before you begin
flinging stones, pray ask yourself a question or two.
Consider if the same thing, under other names, is not
common enough in this highly moral world, among all
grades and conditions of men, and in all trades and pro-
fessions ? It is not on the turf only that sharp men, with
a little more knowledge than their fellows, take advantage
of it to get the best of a deal. The same thing is going on
in every pathway of commerce, and in every walk of life ;

always excepting, of course, those paths of virtue round about Threadneedle Street, in this virtuous city of London.

The Liverpool Cup was one of the races about which there was considerable ante-post betting. The Summer Cup of 1875 produced a " safe 'un " of the safest sort I have ever known ; and furnished the racing world with a sensation and a scandal which is remembered, with bitterness, to the present day. Years ago I was urged to tell the world what I knew about it, and have been offered inducements to do so ; but, for many years, I resisted the temptation. And it was with the greatest reluctance, and only after a trying wrangle with myself on the subject, that I arrived at the conclusion it would be impossible for me to publish these reminiscences of my turf life without some reference to this notorious case, wherein I and my brother, and other near friends were, at the time, and frequently since, charged with complicity. For years after the Fraulein scandal, I and my friends were compelled to submit to pretty constant abuse on the subject, and it was quite a common thing, when we were driving away from a race-course, to be assailed with, " There goes the Fraulein mob," with, occasionally, a very much more violent assortment of epithets ; and yet it is a fact that neither myself, my brother, nor any of the three younger of the quartette of the brothers Collins, had the slightest bit to do with the inception or carrying out of this big job. In fact, not until the very day of the race, and about an hour before it, did either of us suspect anything was wrong with the mare. The truth is, I was on the point

of backing her—although, I must confess, I had been told
not to do so until I got definite orders—when I received my
first intimation that she would probably not be found
among the runners, although she was on the ground. Her
trainer was very confident ; and, I had reason to know,
he and his friends had backed her to win a big stake.

Fraulein had been a good favourite, but, in the language of the turf, she had just begun to smell a bit " fishy,"
and when I settled down to my business of making a book
on the race, I found it a difficult matter to lay a fair share
of it against this mare.

Among others of my regular clients, good old George
Payne came up.

" Now, Mr. Dyke, what will you lay me your Brummagem horse?" meaning, of course, Fraulein.

" I'll bet you four ponies, Mr. Payne," I replied.

" Put it down," he answered.

" Make it four fifties, Mr. Payne."

" I'll see you —— first, Master Dykey," was his answer ;
and as he turned away, added : " She oughtn't to be half
the price if she's a right one."

In a few minutes Mr. Payne returned.

" Your friend Gomm's mare goes badly," said he.
" I suppose I've thrown my pony away, eh, Mr. Dyke ?
You ought to know something about it, eh ? "

Well, I could not tell him what I knew, or rather what
I had reason to suspect ; but having the greatest respect
for this grand old sportsman, I could not refrain from
dropping a hint of it.

" I'd have a pony on Tam o' Shanter if I were you, Mr. Payne," I answered.

" Well, what will you lay me him ? " he asked.

" As you have backed what you consider a ' wrong 'un ' sir, I'll lay you the same price—four ponies, Mr. Payne."

" Done ! I'll have four fifties," he replied quickly.

" No, sir ; I'll only lay the odds to twenty-five pounds," I answered ; and as that horse was at the time a better favourite than Fraulein, I thought I was treating him liberally.

So the two transactions I had with him on the race cost me seventy-five pounds. But, although I would lay him no more myself, I saw him busy among the bookies ; and I fancy he took advantage of the hint I had dropped to a considerable extent.

As far as my memory serves me, it was about twenty minutes before the time set for the race, when a friend of Mr. Gomm's walked into the weighing-room, and delivered into the proper hands that famous letter, signed by the owner of Fraulein, and which ordered his mare to be scratched for the Liverpool Cup. That gentleman's own trainer protested ; everybody present was indignant, and cried " Shame ! " But it was all useless.

Fraulein's number did not go up, and some three or four people won a big sum of money, which the public lost without even getting a run for it. The fact of leaving the mare in the race up to almost the last moment, and squeezing out of the public the last shilling, intensified the indignation of the whole racing community, which the sporting press of the country voiced in language more vigorous than polite toward the authors of the scandal. A very old and dear friend of my own came in for the biggest share of it, while Mr. Gomm himself was not spared. Gomm long since departed this life, in more senses than one a broken man ; but how much of the blame he got was really deserved, there is, I believe, now no man living who could tell.

The following facts, however, will I know stand uncontradicted.

Some time before the Liverpool Races Mr. Gomm gave this old friend of mine an order to back Fraulein for a large amount, limiting him to a price which any sane man should have known it would be impossible to obtain. With this big order he handed my friend the letter authorising the scratching of the mare—in the event of this tremendous order not being carried out—at what time he should think most opportune.

The hour my ancient friend thought most opportune was some twenty minutes before the time the public was expecting the mare's number to go up for the race.

In the meantime a notable bookmaker in Manchester, still alive, another in Newcastle-on-Tyne, another in London, Dan Laurence in the Midlands, Timson & Carr in Birmingham, and others elsewhere, had been busy laying against her. This much I know for a fact ; and I always held an opinion that the long-headed Staffordshire collier was the prime mover in the whole business. That Fraulein would have won her backers' money had she been permitted to run was amply demonstrated when two days later she cantered away with a race almost as important as the Cup ; and again when a few months later she won the Doncaster Cup with nearly nine stone on her back.

And so ends for ever as far as I am concerned this painful episode, which, if I could, I would gladly have left untouched.

I come now to another highly sensational case—the disqualification of Pattern, wherein I suppose I must consider myself chief actor ; for the disqualification of that horse, for all the races he had ever won, was brought about by myself. The case at that time caused a great sensation and brought me, from certain people who happened to suffer by it, a plentiful crop of abuse and ill-will ; the amusing part of the business was, however, that those who howled loudest being a little hurt were all such as would only too gladly have assisted at it, if they had known as much as I did anent this matter. In fact, I question if the sting of being left out of such a good thing was not, with some of them, more painful than losing their money.

In the year 1885 Pattern ran twelve times, winning six races. It was I think in the spring of that year when I got my first inkling of the fact that those responsible for entering him for all these races were getting an unfair advantage over all their opponents to the extent of some pounds in every race he ran in ; the fact being he was a year older than they claimed him to be. And now before

I proceed any farther let me frankly admit that I do not believe—what I have more than once heard insinuated —that there was anything like a fraud intended.   I am quite certain Mr. Young Graham who bred the horse, and who was I believe all through his actual owner, would never have countenanced such a thing, nor have I any reason to suppose that Dr. Dougall, who managed him under a lease, had the slightest idea that he was wrongly describing him when he entered him as a five-year-old, while he was really a six-year-old.

Up to the present time the whole of the facts of the case have never been published and that is what I now propose doing.   For my own share in these transactions, whatever blame belongs to me I am willing to bear ;   and, judged by the general standard of morality I am aware I shall be considered blamable, but judged by the ethics of the turf and its common practice I must be acquitted.   I am certain I did nothing that any ordinary followers of racing would not have done in similar circumstances.

I do not intend to disclose the exact means by which I received the first hint of the fraud which was being perpetrated, and which, for all I knew at the time, might not have been so innocent as I now believe it to have been ; to do so would possibly do an injury to a person still actively engaged on the turf.

I need not tell the brotherhood of bookmakers or indeed any human being acquainted with the turf and its practices that the moment I became possessed of the valuable asset contained in this knowledge I did not share it with everybody I met. According to ordinary morals, that is of course what I ought to have done ; instead of which, however, I carefully locked up the knowledge until such time as it might be of use to myself and the friends whom I might see fit to enlighten.

The thing I set myself to do was to wait patiently until I should find Pattern a red-hot favourite, then lay my little pile against him. He ran a good many times, but never, when I was present, was he such a favourite as would make it worth my while acting against him.

At the Shrewsbury meeting he was in a Hunter's Flat Race when I thought the time had surely come, and I went there prepared to bring off the good thing. On the book it appeared good for him to beat all the known performers ; but there arrived on the scene a certain unknown candidate, a grand-looking black horse belonging to Mr. Fowler, and trained by Sam Darling. Just before the race Mr. Best, one of the principal patrons of the stable and one of the most astute men I have met on the turf, took me into a quiet corner.

" I want you to put a bit of money for the stable," he said, " on one of ours in the next race."

" With pleasure, Mr. Best," I replied. " Bloodstone is the horse, I presume ; how much do you want on ? "

" Well, I cannot tell you the exact amount," he answered, "but get all the long prices you can, and go on till I tell you to stop. I'll be near you."

I could see this was a big job, and coming from such a quarter, no doubt an absolute " cert." So I ventured to remind my astute friend that he should not expect too much ; as Shrewsbury was no longer the Shrewsbury of John Frail and the old times, when you could have put two or three thousand on a horse, and then not make him a favourite ; the market now was poor and weak and the big black horse was sure to be a good favourite when three or four hundred pounds had been invested ; and I then added :

" He is in at Derby next week you say, Mr. Best ; why not keep him till then ?   You may win as many thousands there as hundreds here and perhaps with no greater outlay."   This advice, however, was of no avail.

" The horse is here," he said, " and must take his chance."

I saw it was all over with any possibility of seeing Pattern a favourite so I made up my mind to " field " on the race for Bloodstone, and allow Pattern to wait for another day.   Of course with the knowledge I had of Bloodstone I may have laid something extra against Pattern, but with no idea of getting him disqualified, as was in after days more than once asserted by my old and esteemed friend, " Toney " Benjamin, who happened on that occasion to subscribe to my book, I believe, a matter of five-and-twenty pounds.

Well, Bloodstone won very easily, as he was bound to do, considering he was receiving a lump of weight from horses to whom he could readily have conceded as much.

So we arrive at December, 1885, and unless the *coup* can be brought off before the end of the month, all my knowledge and patient waiting will have been thrown away, for on the first day of another month he will be, according to the book, an aged horse, and he will thenceforth be carrying his correct weight.

I saw he was entered at Kempton Park and I fervently hoped Dr. Dougall would run him ; for it was not only, in all probability, the last opportunity I should have, but his opponents in this race were but a middling lot, with old Beckhampton perhaps the best of them ; so if the field should not be too numerous it might be a case of odds on ; and with this, given a good market, what possibilities loomed before me !

When the day arrived it seemed as though all the forces of nature were arrayed against me and after all I should be baulked of my prey. It hailed, rained and snowed, and there had been a sharp frost during the night. " No racing to-day," I said to myself, " and perhaps not for many days and so end my golden hopes in this direction."

However I went down to Waterloo Station to try to ascertain whether there would be racing. There were very few people there and among them great diversity of opinion on the subject. No authoritative message arrived so some went home again. I and a mere handful of others went down to Kempton on the off-chance. We found there a very miserable attendance with still a doubt as to whether there would be any racing.

At last the stewards decided to give it a trial, and with danger and difficulty the three first races were brought off ;

and then the numbers were hoisted for Pattern's race, and my eyes were gladdened to see that animal's number among them, accompanied by Beckhampton, Maid of the Mill and Quite Too Too ; so I was satisfied that Pattern would be a strong favourite ; and one of the right sort of " safe 'uns " to lay against ; but the unfortunate condition of the market was not promising for anything big being done. I tried hurriedly to find Tom Leader so as to impress upon him the necessity of his jockey persevering with his old horse so as to make sure of being in front of the two outsiders—which I knew he would be certain to do unless he should be pulled up in the event of Pattern appearing to have the race in hand— my intention being to back Beckhampton heavily instead of laying against Pattern, which would come to much the same thing without exposing me to quite so much notice. In this however I was foiled as Mr. Leader was not to be found ; so I commenced to make a one-horse book, laying all I could against Pattern.

The gentlemanly element of the turf was almost entirely absent, and I could see that all my customers would be the hard-headed sharps of the ring. My clerk not being with me I begged the genial Tom Collins to wield the pencil for me on this one race. The clever division rushed to lay the odds on Pattern and I accommodated them as fast as they came ; and when Mr. Fry and some others of the few fielders present began to hold out for increased odds I continued to accommodate them at about the old rate, and friend Tom looked aghast.

" Do you know what you're doing ? " he asked with dismay. " You'll lose a heap of money if Pattern wins."

" No, I shan't," was my reply. " You go on writing all I lay and ask no questions."

Of course he then understood I had a reason for what I was doing.

They are off ! Up the straight the four horses come ! Pattern, as my friends afterwards told me, leading many a length. I had no care for the horses ; I did not see them ; nor did I want to see them. My back was turned to them and my face toward the hard-heads on the stand who thought they were besting me while still my cry rang out :

" I'll take two to one ! "

" Me a pony ! " " Me a pony ! " and " Me fifty ! " shouts out excitedly and at the same instant such innocents as Arthur Cooper, Teddy Hobson, and John O'Neil. And down went these amounts with many others.

The race is over and Pattern is acclaimed the winner. I rushed instantly to the weighing-room, arranged with Leader for an objection, and then the fun began again— this time in the paddock.

The doctor himself came up.

" What do you suppose you know about my horse ? " he asked through his clenched teeth.

" I know enough to take you three ponies you don't get the race," I answered.

" Done ! " said he.

And " Done ! " " Done ! " " Done ! " came again from

the same old set, who might be excused for believing that the doctor knew more of his own horse than I could possibly know. So there was ultimately almost as much money betted after the race as before it.

Well, the objection on the question of wrong age and therefore carrying short weight was duly gone into by the stewards, and Pattern promptly disqualified.

This decision was more disastrous and far-reaching in its results than I had intended or dreamt of, for it necessitated the horse's disqualification for every one of the six races he had won throughout the year. The second horse in all these races was declared the winner; stakes and bets were ordered to be refunded. Law-suits and trouble of other sort for which I was sincerely sorry ensued, and there was any quantity of excitement about the case in racing circles. Losers on the race refused to pay up; those who had won by Pattern on previous races protested against having to disgorge, and there was great difficulty in recovering the stakes which had been unjustly won. There was much printer's ink wasted 'twixt leading articles and vehement correspondence, and altogether such a stir made that ultimately the racing authorities were compelled to so far modify the rules as to prevent future disqualifications from having such a retrospective penalty.

It was most unfortunate for Captain Middleton, Dr. Dougall, and those who suffered with them on this occasion that Pattern's race was not later on the card, because immediately after it, the ground becoming rapidly more dangerous, the stewards ordered the racing to be discontinued.

Those who had lost most money to me declined to settle until they had consulted the highest authority on the subject, so I was summoned at the instance of Dr. Dougall to appear before the Committee of Tattersalls. And for the purpose of hearing the case there was a very full meeting of that august and important body, with the Duke of Beaufort in the chair. Dr. Dougall was first called upon for his version of the affair and then three or four of his fellow-sufferers. Finally I was called up for my defence and to make a short story of it I may say I came out with flying colours and they were ordered to pay, which with one solitary exception, and that for a very small amount, every one did. Prince Soltykoff, as I was about to leave the room put the whole case in a nutshell :

" You were betting, I suppose, Dyke, on what you thought you knew," said the Prince.

" That was so," I replied, and then the Prince added :

" Evidently those gentlemen were betting on what they thought they knew, only your knowledge on this occasion happened to be the better."

My readers, I am sure, will be wondering how it came about that a horse could be entered in such a lot of races, run in a dozen of them, winning no less than six of the stakes, and this happening all over the country and extending throughout one entire season, the horse all the while wrongly described in the vital matter of age and therefore always carrying short weight—and no one of the clever people who are always on the look-out for such opportunities becoming aware of the fact.

Without a true understanding of the case it seems impossible to exonerate from blame certain people, especially the breeder and owner and perhaps another nearly concerned in the management of the horse.

Here then are the simple facts of the case. Pattern began his inglorious career in public almost as early as it was possible for him to do so, which was in the Cup for two-year-olds, at Lincoln, March 23rd, 1881 ; poor Archie Wainwright riding him. He ran again at the Newmarket Second Spring meeting in a two-year-old plate, this time Charley Wood being his jockey. Running very badly on the two first attempts it was decided to trust him no more till such time as the Nurseries were about ; so we find him running his next race—and his last as a two-year-old—in the Loudoun Nursery at the Derby September meeting, and here he showed no improvement on his wretched performances in the early part of the year ; hence his owner in disgust turned him out of training and tried to forget such a horse had been foaled— the tragic part of the business for Dr. Dougall, and many others, being that the owner forgot too much ; so that when he had been thrown on one side for nearly three years, and everybody, including Mr. Graham, had well-nigh forgotten him, some wretched groom did that gentleman the ill-turn of reminding him of the horse's existence, intimating at the same time that he looked after all like making a racehorse. So he was fetched up, groomed and

U

then put into training, and by and by the time arrived to enter him in a race and then ensued the tragic part of the matter.

Time had gone I suppose so pleasantly with my friend Mr. Young Graham that he counted the three years Pattern had been " turned up " as two ; entering him as a five-year-old instead of six, neither Mr. Graham nor anybody else taking the simple precaution of testing memory by a glance at the Stud Book. So originated this hubbub and trouble and terrible loss for Messrs. Dougall, Graham, Middleton, and a host of others.

CONCLUSION

In bringing these rambling and disjointed reminiscences to an end the thought is borne in upon me that it were better I had set myself to write " a plain, unvarnished tale " of my own life. A good deal of the space given to some of the racing and racing men might, perhaps, have been more usefully occupied in recording many startling incidents in my early business struggle. I have told of my folly in throwing away a magnificent business, with the prospects of a brilliant future. I could have told what might have been more interesting, how, while but a mere youth, and starting with a capital of less than £100, I built up, in two years, a big business with a profitable turnover of towards £20,000 a year. My life as a commercial traveller, during the few years I was so occupied was full of adventure, and although it is nearly fifty years since folly drove me from it, I can recall with perfect vividness many of the episodes of " the road," and the strange characters I met with there. I met factors' travellers who were on the road in the late years of the eighteenth century, and some I knew well, hailing from Birmingham, in my own line, who had commenced very early in the nineteenth. The etiquette and usages of the commercial room even in my time, and the quaint survival of the travellers of an earlier time were, to me, extremely interesting ; and some of the expedients which enabled me to hold my own and occasionally to get a bit in front of these old hands, in dealing with the retail jewellers down in the Far West, were useful to me and very amusing, however much they failed to be appreciated by the old hands.

As soon as racing procured me the means, and throughout nearly the whole of my long racing career, I was engaged in various commercial undertakings, some of them of very considerable dimensions, and I had running at one time a manufactory employing, I suppose, about 150 workers ; an S.P. office doing a very large business ; a weekly newspaper for which I was doing a good deal of the writing ; I was director of two public companies ; I was an active member of a Board of Guardians, a Rural Sanitary Authority, and a local Board of Health—all of which are now in the city of Birmingham, and in addition to all these occupations my chief business was in the betting ring at race meetings, where I was to be found three or four days in every week during the flat racing season. Of course, as I have now good reason to know, my interests were at the mercy of too many people, and as a dear old lady, much wiser than myself, often told me, I had " too many irons in the fire at one time."

During the whole of my long life I have always tried to avoid getting into law, and I have had no great fondness for lawyers ; but even in this prosaic class, where one could scarcely expect to find it, I have known some lovable and interesting people, and some—well, otherwise; many of them having afforded me opportunities for the study of human nature of a widely divergent character. Here I have discovered the grandest example of the really honest man I have ever met, and here, also, the world's greatest " crook."

I believe I could find material for a volume out of my experience of public companies. The proceedings of more than one of them would afford reading of a startling sort; while the origin, history, and " winding up " of another would make " copy " for an extraordinary romance, one which should shake up some good folks in highly respectable commercial and professional atmospheres, which ought to—and possibly may—get itself written some day.

Coming to recent times, even during the ten years of my quiet and almost secluded life in this historically interesting old-world village of Highgate, I have been able to continue my study of human nature, although, naturally, my opportunities are somewhat more limited; yet here, among my few acquaintances and fewer dear friends, I have found specimens worthy the careful study of a psychologist, and if two of them could be lifted, life-like, into the pages of a novel they would make the fortunes of another Dickens.

They tell me I am an old man. I don't want to believe it, and scarcely can I do so; I feel so young, and it seems such a very little time since I really was so; yet as I toss in the air a bonnie member of my family belonging to the fourth generation, or when I am reminded that I began my working life seventy years ago, and was a bound apprentice years before the last of the " hungry forties," I am, perforce, driven to the conclusion there must be some truth in it.

INDEX

PRINTED BY
IRVINE AND CO., LIMITED, 19, BUCKINGHAM STREET, STRAND,
LONDON, W.C.

Milton Keynes UK
Ingram Content Group UK Ltd.
UKHW051008250424
441751UK00007B/291

9 781535 810609